Meditations of a Hedge Fund Manager

MEDITATIONS OF A HEDGE FUND MANAGER

Inspired Insights on Purpose & Prosperity

AARON L. SMITH

XULON ELITE

Xulon Press Elite
2301 Lucien Way #415
Maitland, FL 32751
407.339.4217
www.xulonpress.com

Edited by Xulon Press.

Printed in the United States of America.

ISBN-13: 978-1-54564-059-3

Soli Deo gloria

For my wife, Caro, who has supported me in all my endeavors. She is so kind, compassionate, smart, and full of encouragement. Her laughter is infectious. She has seen me at my very worst but stood by me and loved me anyway. Thank you for making me a better man. *Je t'aime, ma chérie.*

> ***Who can find a virtuous wife? For her worth is far above rubies. The heart of her husband safely trusts her; so he will have no lack of gain.***
>
> ***Strength and honor are her clothing; she shall rejoice in time to come. She opens her mouth with wisdom, and on her tongue is the law of kindness.***
>
> (Proverbs 31:10-11, 25-26)

About the Author

Aaron L. Smith is the founder and majority shareholder of a private US investment management firm. Mr. Smith is a member in good standing of the National Futures Association and holds the series 3 license. Prior to founding his own firm, he served as an executive at a multi-billion dollar systematic global macro hedge fund. Mr. Smith managed licensed financial companies in New York, Singapore and Hong Kong. Mr. Smith began his career at Morgan Stanley in New York's World Trade Center and studied finance and international business at the Leonard N. Stern School of Business at NYU. He resides in Zürich, Switzerland with his beautiful wife Caro and two daughters. When he's not busy looking over institutional portfolios, Aaron loves to ski, mountain bike and teach Sunday school.

Contact Aaron Smith at info@aaronsmith.ch.

Endorsements

"This book is very unique: business smarts with a high level of spiritual insight. I think it is unparalleled and I endorse it fully."

-Daniel Juster,
Founder, Tikkun International (Jerusalem),
Author of "Jewish Roots"

"Aaron Smith is, by my reckoning, one of the rare ones. He's a hedge fund manager and he's a believer. But not just a believer, he's a fully-devoted follower of Christ who isn't shy about speaking his faith boldly to others, something he does regularly, with passion and insight."

-Rev. Douglas J. Brouwer,
Senior Pastor (retired),
International Protestant Church of Zürich,
Author of "How to Become a Multicultural Church"

"The most daring spiritual and real-life insights I ever read from a financial expert."

-Christian Takushi MA UZH,
Macro Economist,
Geopolitical Economics AG, Zürich

"In **Meditations of a Hedge Fund Manager** you will find wisdom and practical advice from a man whose heart is to experience God in his calling as an investment professional in Zürich, Switzerland. You will gain many nuggets of spiritual and professional truths that you can apply in your own life to help you succeed in your calling. I encourage every marketplace leader to read Aaron's excellent work!"

-Os Hillman,
President of Marketplace Leaders LLC,
Author of "TGIF Today God is First"

"If you're looking for a book to guide you through the perils and obstacles of the marketplace, then this book is a must read. Aaron Smith, a leading hedge fund manager, has masterfully shared the secrets of success discovered through a life submitted to God and Scripture. As a result this book is a brilliant resource for marketplace professionals. Aaron's vulnerability and wisdom will be a torch on your pathway to success, not just in business but in life.

-Ryan Waters,
Senior Pastor, C3 Mumbai

"**Meditations of a Hedge Fund Manager** is a compelling message from a writer who takes care to walk closely with the Lord Jesus. His desire is to share with all who seek the truth and purpose in life in the person of Jesus. Being a Christian in the competitive work and business environment, Aaron is able to communicate with conviction how Christians in the workplace should align themselves to an eternal perspective."

-Eric Choa,
CEO & Director,
Elpis Financial (Singapore) Pte. Ltd.

Contents

Preface

The pages ahead are intended to be uplifting, yet serious. It is my hope that you will read them with an open mind and open heart. Writing these Meditations has taken me well outside of my "comfort zone" and will challenge you as well. This book has the potential to be powerful and paradigm shifting in your life, regardless of your faith background.

> ***"And my God shall supply all your need according to His riches in glory by Christ Jesus."*** (Philippians 4:19)

To what or whom are you looking for your supply? Can you believe God to meet even your deepest needs? The context of the above Scripture refers to financial resources, but God's grace overflows to every realm. The Lord has an abundant supply for all of your needs, whether they be financial, physical healing, or emotional wholeness. God's ability and desire to be your supply is forever memorialized in His divine name, Jehovah Jireh.

This name was revealed at the time of Abraham's test, when he willingly gave up Isaac. ***"And Abraham called the name of the place, The-Lord-Will-Provide (Jehovah Jireh); as it is said to this day, 'In the Mount of the Lord it shall be provided.'"*** (Genesis 22:14)

God's provision of the sacrifice in place of Isaac is a prophetic act. To what does the prophecy point? What shall be provided at the Mount of the Lord? Our Lord Jesus climbed that mountain and gave Himself as the ultimate sacrifice. ***"He who did not spare His own Son, but delivered Him up for us***

all, how s hall He not with Him also freely give us all things?" (Romans 8:32)

Faith precedes manifestation. Otherwise, it wouldn't be faith, it would be sight.

> ***"For we walk by faith, not by sight."*** (2 Corinthians 5:7)

> ***"Therefore I say to you, whatever things you ask when you pray, believe that you receive them, and you will have them."*** (Mark 11:24)

How many of us have the order wrong? We might say in our heart, "If I only had such and such, I would believe." We shall not test the Lord in this way, ***"for whatever is not from faith is sin."*** (Romans 14:23)

Below are five Scriptural disciplines that you can immediately employ to walk in *total victory* by *grace* through *faith.* Implementing these disciplines will make the book more impactful.

1. ***HEAR. "Therefore take heed how you hear."*** (Luke 8:18) Pay attention to what you listen to. You are responsible for what you hear. Words are like seeds planted in the heart; the Word of God is the good seed. As the Word is mixed with faith, a bountiful harvest is sure to come. The negative words of the world are also seeds but they bear thorns and thistles. What are you listening to? Turn off the boob tube. Take a sabbatical from social media. Gently deal with that person who is constantly putting doubt and unbelief into your heart. Most people are passive in what they hear, which is a recipe for disaster with the advent of the twenty-four-hour news cycle. Make a conscious decision to listen to wholesome, positive words.

2. ***THINK. "For as he thinks in his heart, so is he."*** (Proverbs 23:7) Meditate on what you think. Thought displacement is the practice of consciously surveying your thought life, recognizing negative or evil thoughts and immediately replacing them with positive, uplifting thoughts. "***Finally, brethren, whatever things are true, whatever things are noble, whatever things are just, whatever things are pure, whatever things are lovely, whatever things are of good report, if there is any virtue and if there is anything praiseworthy—meditate on these things."*** (Philippians 4:8)

3. ***SPEAK. "Death and life are in the power of the tongue."*** (Proverbs 18:21) If you have a pulse, you may struggle with controlling your thoughts as suggested in point two. Suppose one day at work you have a negative thought about a colleague who was openly hostile to your proposal at the last board meeting. Immediately, put thought displacement into practice and start blessing your contrary colleague in your mind. The negative thought will be pushed out of your mind with a positive one, but which thought will win out? The tiebreaker goes to the thought you speak! Lock yourself in the bathroom and start speaking life over your colleague, blessing him, and thanking God for his life.

   When you think evil toward a co-worker, he can sense it. You might not say a word, but it's written on your face. It's like how a wild animal can smell fear. However, when you speak blessing over him and think good towards him, he will also feel it. You will be surprised how your colleague subconsciously warms to you.

   Later that afternoon, your colleague comes over to your desk and says, "Hey, I'm sorry I was so harsh in the meeting this morning. I had a big fight with my wife last night and my son has the flu. Perhaps I overreacted in the meeting. Sorry for that."

"Let no corrupt word proceed out of your mouth, but what is good for necessary edification, that it may impart grace to the hearers." (Ephesians 4:29) The Greek word for corrupt is not limited to curse words but includes useless words. Our words are to impart grace, which is unmerited favor. Therefore, we should not speak to others on the basis of what they deserve, but rather let our words be a conduit of God's grace.

4. ***PRAY. "Therefore I say to you, whatever things you ask when you pray, believe that you receive them, and you will have them."*** (Mark 11:24) Prayer is the channel by which God's grace is actualized in your life. A Swiss newspaper recently reported a survey showing that only four percent of people pray on a daily basis, while fifty-seven percent said they did not pray at all. Ever. Make a plan now to pray in a disciplined, regular way over the week ahead. This is not to impose a legalistic regimen on you. You don't have to pray, you get to pray. In the temple periods, there were regular times ordained throughout the day to help Israel embrace a disciplined prayer life. You can think all the positive thoughts, speak out all the blessings until your throat is hoarse, but remember: God is the source! Therefore, seek Him in prayer.

   It is good to start out with a disciplined regimen like Daniel, who prayed morning, noon, and night. Over time, it will become effortless for you to ***"pray without ceasing."*** (1 Thessalonians 5:17) Personally, I find it especially helpful to pray immediately upon waking before my feet hit the floor as I get out of bed. This sets the tone for the day. Perhaps more importantly, pray before you fall asleep. Don't feel bad if you fall asleep in the middle of the prayer; the Father loves nothing more than when his children fall asleep in His arms. I believe these positive thoughts are being transmitted from your spirit to your soul all night, ***"for he provides for his beloved, even when they sleep."*** (Psalm 127:2, CJB)

5. ***IMAGINE.*** A picture is worth a thousand words. Your imagination is extremely powerful and creative. Many people's imaginations are dominated by fear. ***"For the thing I greatly feared has come upon me, and what I dreaded has happened to me."*** (Job 3:25) Instead of letting your imagination run wild with anxieties and fears, rest your hope in the confident expectation of God's goodness. Visualize right actions, wholeness, peace and prosperity. Be as detailed as possible in the process. Every building started as a picture in the mind of the architect. In the same way, visualize the expected end intended by the Lord.

These simple methods (Hear, Think, Speak, Pray, and Imagine) will bless you immensely. Begin practicing these methods as you read the following meditations.

Meditation I

Purpose: Fulfilling your Destiny

"The steps of a good man are ordered by the Lord, and He delights in his way." (Psalm 37:23)

As the nurse removed the IV drip from my arm, I proceeded to check out of NYU Medical Center and jumped into a taxi heading downtown. I was still sick to my stomach from the effects of salmonella food poisoning after eating some bad sushi the day before at Astor Place. My stomach churned as the yellow cab jostled in and out of New York City morning rush hour traffic. As I laid my head back and closed my eyes, a terrible burning smell wafted through the vents. NYC taxis are notorious for assaulting one's sense of smell, but this was something completely different. The air smelled like burning metal. As we headed further south, the traffic came to a standstill. All around us, thousands of people were covered in ash, walking north. Men and women in business suits, grey from head to toe.

I should have been at my office that morning. I was so proud to work on the seventy-third floor of New York City's World Trade Center. I had never missed a day of work or come in late.

What I didn't realize was those people I was seeing were fleeing from the first attack on the continental US since the War of 1812. Earlier that morning, a Boeing 767 had struck the south tower just a few floors above where I worked.

Of all the times to get food poisoning, I managed to get it at precisely the right moment before the attacks of September 11, 2001. Looking back, what I sensed even then is so clear to me now: that there is a purpose for our lives. Now, I do not mean to imply that those who died that day did not have a purpose. On the contrary, I know many examples first-hand of those who fulfilled their purpose in the most noble and selfless way, giving their lives to save others during the attacks. Nonetheless, I couldn't help coming away from the experience knowing that there was a call on my life. I felt this again on November 26, 2008. That fateful day, I suddenly had a severe slipped disc in my neck which prevented me from checking into the Taj hotel in Mumbai as scheduled. I had specifically requested a room in the old colonial wing of the hotel, exactly where the terror cell based its operations. I narrowly avoided death a second time. That day, the Taj was bombed by Islamic terrorists. Six explosions went off, killing 164 and severely wounding 308. Once again, my life was spared from tragic events.

Salmonella and a slipped disc. Perhaps these are coincidences? Or could it be . . . divine protection? George Washington, the first president of the United States, is said to have believed that he could not die until his purpose in life had been achieved. His courage as a general in the Revolutionary War and the French and Indian War is legendary. He took extreme risks in battle, including one time where his coat was riddled with bullet holes.

Years later, an Indian chief recounted this battle and told Washington he realized he had divine protection and ordered his braves to stop firing at Washington. He then went on to prophesy that Washington would become the father of a great nation. Like Washington, when we discover the purpose of our life, we will ignore adverse circumstances and focus on the big picture. Having a vision for our purpose in life will enable us to have the courage and integrity to step out and achieve great things.

Our purpose transcends the daily spin-cycle of eat, work, sleep, repeat. We each have a destiny, each of us possess an opportunity to develop an eternal legacy established in our hearts before we were born, for we are ***"fearfully and***

wonderfully made." (Psalm 139:14) Deep down, most of us, if we care to admit it, yearn for greatness. We know intuitively that there must be more to life than just surviving. The hunger we have for something greater than daily survival indicates a possibility of fulfilment.

Bill Johnson of Redding, California expresses it like this: "Written into the spiritual DNA of every believer is an appetite for the impossible that cannot be ignored or wished away . . . Our hearts know that there is much more to life than what we perceive with our senses."[1] In a natural sense, our appetite, the presence of hunger, indicates the possibility of eating and being filled. In the same way, our spiritual hunger is satiated as we discover and execute God's purpose for our life.

> ***"'For I know the plans I have for you,' declares the Lord, 'plans to prosper you and not to harm you, plans to give you a hope and future.'"*** (Jeremiah 29:11 NIV)

This is one of the most quoted verses in Scripture and for good reason. Deep inside, each of us intuitively knows we are not in control of our life. Yes, we try to make good decisions, employ healthy disciplines, and do our best to avoid dangers. Yet, if we are honest, we know the greatest triumphs and the worst disasters are far beyond our control. Terrorism, natural disasters, stage four cancer. So many things are beyond our control that we find great comfort in the fact that there is an all-powerful God, and that we can know Him personally. The Bible goes so far as to show us that we can know God so intimately that we may call him Father. Jesus Christ called him Abba, the most affectionate term possible in the vernacular. Our Papa, we might say.

While Jeremiah 29:11 shows our Papa has a plan for our lives, verses 12-13 show how this purpose is to be fulfilled:

---

[1] *The Supernatural Power of a Transformed Mind,* Bill Johnson

"Then you shall come and call upon me and pray to me. Then you shall seek me and find me when you seek me with all of your heart."

This is the part that is often overlooked. It's comforting to know there is a good plan for our lives but let's not ignore our personal responsibility in fulfilling that plan. I am convinced the key to achieving our divine purpose is simply to seek Him with all our heart. As we seek Him, everything else will fall into place. This is the essence of ***"seek first the kingdom of God and His righteousness, and all these things shall be added to you."*** (Matthew 6:33) The command to seek Him is connected to the promise that all the necessary things will be added. As we start moving toward the Kingdom, God will intercept us on the journey and manifest in our relationships and work-life. And He will supply all the resources and connections necessary to fulfill His purpose.

UNLOCK THE POWER OF INFINITY

It is critical that we look to the Lord for our purpose. As the prophet Jeremiah says: ***"O Lord, I know the way of man is not in himself; it is not in man who walks to direct his own steps."*** (Jeremiah 10:23) When we try to discern our purpose for ourselves, we easily get off course by emotions, pressures, parental influence, and other external factors. This is where the Word of God comes in. We need to have an objective, absolute standard of truth outside of ourselves. The Word establishes the general calling and purpose for all believers. These are enumerated in the Great Commission (Matthew 28:18-20) and other commandments written in the New Covenant.

So, we start with the Word of God as our objective foundation for finding our purpose and meaning in life. In order to find more specific information, we need to go deeper into a relationship with the Lord. After all, the point of the Book is to introduce us to the Author. In seeking the Lord with all our heart, every single person on the planet is on the path to discovering their own divine destiny, which will unlock great meaning and purpose not only for themselves, but for their community as well.

Perhaps you are looking around and find yourself unable to see anyone who appears to have found their purpose in life, let alone achieved fulfilment. The fact that few people ever realize their potential does not diminish the possibility of finding and achieving it. Just think of electricity. Countless generations of humans lived in darkness for ages, with the only illumination being firelight. Just because for most of human existence no one experienced the benefit of electricity does not mean the potential to tame it was not there. The physical properties that enabled Edison to power a light bulb have been present since creation. The potential to unlock its secrets was always there, just waiting for the right person. Just because most, if not all, people around you are walking in futility doesn't mean that you can't start discovering your purpose today. It's been there all the time, just waiting to be discovered!

EMPOWERED TO FULFILL YOUR DESTINY

A tree was created to reproduce other trees. There may be secondary benefits, such as giving shade and providing fruit for us to eat, but growth and multiplicity are embedded into every seed. This is the essence of the Kingdom of God; the word is likened to a seed. In seeking Him first, we become fruitful and unlock our potential.

> ***"But his delight is in the law of the Lord, and in His law he meditates day and night. He shall be like a tree planted by the rivers of water, that brings forth its fruit in its season, whose leaf also shall not wither; and whatever he does shall prosper."*** (Psalm 1:2-3)

Have you ever seen a tree strive to bear fruit? It doesn't struggle or strain; it is something that comes naturally in due season. Sometimes, during dry seasons, a tree may only produce a limited amount of fruit, but it still produces something. The key to producing fruit abundantly is for the tree to have been planted by the river. When we meditate and focus on God's Word, it's like being replanted on the river bank and we can start bearing fruit effortlessly.

Sight says, "This is just an acorn," whereas faith says, "Here are a million oak trees." Everything about the tree was designed to bring forth increase. Everything about you is designed to enable you to fulfil a purpose. Our Papa first thought about you in eternity past. Let's consider eternity for a moment. With all the noise of our daily lives, including the twenty-four-hour news cycles, we rarely stop to consider a concept like the infinite nature of eternity. In actuality, eternity is not just a big question—it is the only question. Mathematically speaking, any number divided by infinity is zero. Now assume the worst possible life with a typical lifespan of eighty years. Eighty divided by infinity equals zero. Therefore, the worst possible life would literally be nothing compared to eternal paradise. As finite creatures, the concept of timelessness is difficult for us to grasp. We are like fish which are born, live, and die in water. Fish have no other frame of reference about any life outside of the body of water they live in. To them, the whole world is like this.

God is infinite and eternal. For Him, no temporal gain could be great enough to justify the smallest loss in eternity. That's just how the math stacks up. What we need to realize is that nothing is more important than our eternal destiny. As we discover our divine purpose and seek the Lord, each one of us can have an eternal impact. That's breathtaking!

I'm a business person and I like to see practical applications, for I believe truth should be relevant. When we become truly aware of our potential to have an eternal impact, it will have profound implications for our present-day experience. The excitement that comes from this revelation floods our hearts and minds with hope.

Consider this example I heard years ago from Pastor Tim Keller in New York: two old women were consigned to work in a basement sweatshop in Chinatown. Both work in equally squalid conditions with no natural light, poor ventilation, grueling production quotas and long hours. They then go straight back to an apartment with other women where they will eat and sleep, then wake up the next day to repeat the process all over again. The first lady is told if she works consistently, at the end of the year, she will get paid five dollars per hour worked and given the privilege of being able to work another year rather than being deported back to China. The second lady is promised at the end of the year to receive the same wage, but unlike the first woman, she is promised a $1 million bonus and told she will be free to go anywhere in America that she likes.

Notice each lady has to endure the exact same working conditions, but their daily experience could not be more different. Hope changes everything. The first one toils along in hopelessness, her days indescribably long and painful, while the second lady is singing all the time; her days passing by lightly and quickly. Hope has a massive impact on our present reality.

Hope is the vision where our heart sees our eternal purpose being fulfilled. Without a vision of our purpose, we will lean toward merely seeking pleasure and/or avoiding discomfort, for, as the old adage goes, "let us eat, drink and be merry, for tomorrow we die." This is what the Bible describes as the carnal life, merely focused on eating, drinking, obtaining things and immediate gratification.

In the carnal life, success is typically defined by consumption and materialism. I know a self-made billionaire in Geneva who is behind some of the largest natural resource discoveries of the past century. He took incredible risks in frontier markets to achieve his lifelong goal of becoming a billionaire. Among his investments were gold mines in Ecuador, diamond mines in Mozambique, and other commodity projects that were considered incredibly speculative. While others shied away from these markets because they were considered too risky and volatile, he was determined and capable of taking breathtaking risk to achieve his goal, figuring the possibility of reward vastly outweighed the consequences of failure. Finally, all the risk that others were not willing to engage in paid off.

Shortly after his net worth crossed the billion-dollar level, the doctors gave him a tragic report: leukemia. On his deathbed, he told one of my partners, "I would trade every franc I have to live just a bit more." Is there anything sadder than dedicating one's life to the pursuit of a self-centered dream that, even if it brings worldly success, is fleeting and gone in a moment? Most will never achieve the goals that this man did, but those who do reach the pinnacle of power and success soon come to see how hollow it truly is; a cruel mirage in the desert that vanishes before our eyes. As C. Anello, the protagonist in the film, "A Bronx Tale", says, "The saddest thing in life is wasted talent, and the choices you make will shape your life forever."

If the world offers us a counterfeit purpose (such as an insatiable pursuit of wealth for its own sake, lust, greed, power), then it stands to reason that there is a true purpose that can be discerned and achieved. The reason is, a counterfeit means there has to be a valuable original somewhere. As the saying goes, no one counterfeits a two-dollar bill. The original is always superior to the counterfeit, which has flaws in some way that differentiate it from the original. The starting point to the original, your true purpose, is always with God's Word.

> ***"All Scripture is God-breathed and is useful for teaching, rebuking, correcting and training in righteousness, so that the servant of God may be thoroughly equipped for every good work."***
> (2 Timothy 3:16-17)

The Bible is an incredible compilation of books. It contains stunning poetry, historical prose, prophetic visions, parables, and personal correspondence. Its diversity goes beyond mere style, spanning centuries, languages, geographic regions and cultures. The Bible is a complete and authoritative body of work, being divinely inspired or "God-breathed." However, though we work out of a perfect book, sometimes we fail to interpret it correctly or apply it to our lives. Nonetheless, Scripture is pragmatic; it roots the gospel to historical places and verifiable events. The Bible does not present abstract philosophical truths that have no relevance to us today; its teaching may be applied practically and meaningfully to daily life.

I once listened to message from Pastor Derek Prince. I was impressed with the way this man of God carried himself; his tremendous testimonies and the fruit born in his life. I thought to myself: *I want the anointing that man has on his life,* so I continued listening (Prince had already been called home to be with the Lord in glory by that time). He gave a simple testimony of how he had been reading the Bible every day for more than fifty years. On average, he read the Bible cover-to-cover twice per year. He said in unequivocal terms: "You need to do this and it will change your life."

I took his word for it. I reasoned that anyone with fourteen adopted children must at least be sincere. Ever since then, I've been in the word every day. Not because I have to, but because I get to! What a privilege to sit at the feet of the Master: ***"For man does not live by bread alone, but by every word that proceeds from the mouth of God."*** (Matthew 4:4) What a blessing to savor and cherish His every word. What a thrill to search the Scriptures, constantly pouring over His great promises. When I read the Word of God, I'm like a kid at Christmas; I'm excited to unwrap the Word and see what precious fresh and new gifts He has for me every time I open it.

My first cover-to-cover reading took two months. When I read Revelation 22:21, I was so excited that I went back to Genesis 1 and started all over again. Maybe no one ever told you to read your Bible. Well, friend, now I'm telling you, you need to read the Word of God every day.

After you eat a meal, do you tell yourself the next morning, you don't need to eat anymore because you took care of that last night? Of course not; you would starve. Job said, ***"I have esteemed the words of his mouth more than my necessary food."*** (Job 23:12) It is referred to as bread (Matthew 4:4), and honey. (Psalm 119:103, Revelation 10:9-10) I recommend you start with the book of John and go from there. Before you start to read, always take a moment to ask God to open His truths to you. The psalmist said, ***"Open my eyes, that I may see wondrous things from Your law."*** (Psalm 119:18)

Suppose you were reading a book while on an airplane and you happened to learn the author was right next to you. If you came across a section you did not understand, wouldn't you ask the author what he meant in the part you were confused over? We can do the same thing with God. Ask Him to help you understand what you are reading and He will. When you do this, you will find reading the Word of God is not a burden, but the most glorious blessing.

> ***"For the word of God is living and active, sharper than any two-edged sword, piercing to the division of soul and of spirit, of joints and of marrow, and discerning the thoughts and intentions of the heart."*** (Hebrews 4:12)

The below is a list of the benefits of the Word of God.

- God's Word brings true health, fruitfulness, prosperity, and success to what we do. (Psalm 1:3)

- The Word of God has healing power and the power to deliver us from oppression. (Psalm 107:20; Matthew 8:8; Matthew 8:16)

- God's Word cleanses us. If we take heed according to God's Word, our way will be cleansed. (Psalm 119:9; John 15:3; Ephesians 5:26)

- The Word of God, hidden in our hearts, keeps us from sin. (Psalm 119:11)

- God's Word is a counselor. When we delight in God's Word, it becomes a rich source of counsel and guidance for us. (Psalm 119:24)

- God's Word is a source of strength. (Psalm 119:28)

- God's Word imparts life. It is a continual source of life. (Psalm 119:93; Matthew 4:4)

- God's Word is a source of illumination and guidance. When God's Word comes in, light comes in. It makes the simple wise and gives understanding. (Psalm 119:105, 30)

- God's Word gives peace to those who love it. They are secure, standing in a safe place. (Psalm 119:165)

- When the Word of God is heard and understood, it bears fruit. (Matthew 13:23)

- The Word of God has inherent power and authority against demonic power. (Luke 4:36)

- Jesus Himself—His eternal person—is described as the incarnate *Word*. When we are into the Word of God, we are into Jesus. (John 1:1)

- Hearing God's Word is essential to eternal life. One cannot pass from death to life unless they hear the Word of God. (John 5:24; James 1:21; 1 Peter 1:23)

- Abiding—living in—God's Word is evidence of true discipleship. (John 8:31)

- God's Word is the means to sanctification. (John 17:17)

- The Holy Spirit can work with great power as the Word of God is preached. (Acts 10:44)

- Hearing God's Word builds faith. (Romans 10:17)

- Holding fast to the Word of God gives assurance of salvation. (1 Corinthians 15:2)

- The faithful handling of the Word of God gives the ministers of the word a clear conscience. They know that they did all they could before God. (2 Corinthians 4:2; Philippians 2:16)

- The Word of God is the sword of the Spirit. It is equipment for spiritual battle, especially in the idea of an offensive weapon. (Ephesians 6:17)

- The Word of God comes with the power of the Holy Spirit, with "much assurance." (1 Thessalonians 1:5)

- The Word of God works effectively in those who believe it. (1 Thessalonians 2:13)

- The Word of God sanctifies the very food we eat. (1 Timothy 4:5)

- The Word of God is not dead; it is living and active and sharper than any two-edged sword. The Word of God can probe us like a surgeon's expert scalpel, cutting away what needs to be cut and keeping what needs to be kept. (Hebrews 4:12)

- The Word of God is the Christian's source of spiritual growth. (1 Peter 2:2; 1 Corinthians 2:1-5)[2]

One may complain the Word doesn't tell us what do to in many specific cases such as which major to study, which job to choose, which way to drive to work, or which person to marry. The Word doesn't merely tell us what to think, it shows us *how* to think. It doesn't merely provide information and data; it completely revolutionizes the operating system. ***"It is the Spirit who gives life; the flesh profits nothing. The words that I speak to you are spirit, and they are life."*** (John 6:63) The Holy Spirit brings things to our remembrance, guides us into all truth and shows us things to come. That pretty much covers everything we will face in our past, present, and future. Would we expect any less from the Alpha and the Omega?

Let each of us be transformed in the renewing of our mind; the word "transformed" in Romans 12:2 is exactly the same word used to describe the transfiguration of Jesus on the mountain. The Greek word used here is *metamorphóō*, from which we derive "metamorphosis" as in the caterpillar changing into a butterfly (*metá*, "change after being with" and *morphóō*, "changing form in keeping with inner reality") properly, transformed after being with; transfigured.

> ***"Now after six days Jesus took Peter, James, and John, and led them up on a high mountain apart by themselves; and He was transfigured***

---

[2] List compiled by Dan Guzik, www.enduringword.com, which has a helpful online Bible commentary.

> ***before them. His clothes became shining, exceedingly white, like snow, such as no launderer on earth can whiten them."*** (Mark 9:2)

The carnal mind is stuck on the earthly, sensual, and the demonic. Yet, we have the mind of Christ. As we are renewed in our minds by the washing of the Word, we transcend the world, we climb up a high mountain and experience the glory and radiance of His presence! Isn't it awesome? Oh, taste and see! Once we have tasted, once we have beheld Him, shall we again hunger after the world? If we come back down the mountain, it is merely to destroy the works of the devil, to dislodge stubborn demonic forces, to trample scorpions and serpents . . . to do His works, yes, even greater works, because He who is in us is greater!

> ***"And let us run with endurance the race that is set before us."*** (Hebrews 12:11)

In summary, we find a fulfilling life will be achieved when we discover and pursue our God-given purpose. In the Meditations ahead, we will look at how to apply ancient biblical wisdom to achieve true wealth and success.

Prayer: *I thank you, God, that you have a wonderful destiny for my life. Build my faith and remove any hindrance which would prevent me from fulfilling your purpose. I know you have great things in mind, and I set my hope on you. Thank you for your promise that as I seek you, you will reveal yourself to me. In Jesus' name. Amen.*

Meditation II

Avodah: Work as Worship

Whatever your hand finds to do; do it with your might. (Ecclesiastes 9:10)

The "layman" need never think of his humbler task as being inferior to that of his minister. Let every man abide in the calling wherein he is called and his work will be as sacred as the work of the ministry. It is not what a man does that determines whether his work is sacred or secular, it is why he does it. The motive is everything. Let a man sanctify the Lord God in his heart and he can thereafter do no common act. All he does is good and acceptable to God through Jesus Christ. For such a man, living itself will be sacramental and the whole world a sanctuary. His entire life will be a priestly ministration.

-A.W. Tozer, *The Pursuit of God*

Each day presents unique challenges and opportunities to love, believe, forgive, and praise God. The general purpose for all believers is to love and be loved. We are created first and foremost to be objects and recipients of God's love, for it is written, ***"for God is love."*** (1 John 4:8) Furthermore, we are to be executors of His will, given power of attorney to act in His name and on behalf of the Kingdom. This is further illustrated in a title the Apostle Paul gives to Christians: ***"Now then, we are ambassadors for Christ."*** (2 Corinthians 5:20)

An ambassador is appointed by the ruler of a nation to represent him in a foreign country. The ambassador is not there to promote his own agenda. When he appears before government officials in the host country, he has no right to offer his opinion on any aspect of his home country's foreign policy. His primary job is to be essentially a visible copy of the ruler who appointed him. The Bible says we are strangers in this world, for heaven is our home.

> ***"For the gifts and the calling of God are irrevocable."*** (Romans 11:29)

God has designed a specific calling for each individual; then, just as a solider is equipped by the country which sends him into battle, God supplements His calling with gifts and talents that enable us to successfully pursue our calling.

Examples of a calling and the corresponding gifts:

Leader: good at shepherding people, naturally connects with others

Evangelist: outgoing, strong communicator

Administrator: excels in attention to details, well organized

Teacher: highly interested in and skilled in the Word, a creative thinker

Healer: nurturing, emotionally empathetic, supernaturally gifted to heal

Your specific blend of gifts is unique to you. It used to be when preachers talked about a call to service, it primarily referred to a full-time ministry such as the pastorate or Christian school teaching. However, with today's modern technology being so much more powerful compared to that of those who lived over hundred years ago, Christian service can now mean so much more. For example, there are missionaries all over the world who need a full-time pilot or aircraft mechanic. The point is, God can call you to work just about anywhere, so long as it isn't immoral.

Consider Sophia, an investment banker at a large Wall Street firm who works in mergers and acquisitions. Sophia is called to be a healer; she has that imprinted in her spiritual DNA. She has the potential to bring healing to every area of her life, regardless of her specific job or task. It doesn't mean she has to be a medical professional, although that may have been a natural fit for her. It means she brings healing and care in every aspect of her walk, whether it's in a family context as a mother, sister, or daughter, or in a business context. Perhaps in M&A, her calling is expressed as she uses her gifts to turn around situations, bringing healing and care to a struggling business or product line. It can be something as simple as a kind word spoken at just the right time, or even a gesture that heals by bringing encouragement. All the work of her hand is blessed. Whatever she touches becomes a point of contact for the Holy Spirit to flow through and for the Kingdom to be released into the situation.

> "*So God called Moses and David from following the ewes, Elisha from the plough-tail, the apostles from fishing, washing, and mending their nets. He usually appeared to the busy in visions, like as Satan doth to the idle in manifold temptations.*" (John Trapp)

Once we submit control of our lives to Jesus, we are vulnerable in a certain sense because we are no longer in charge of our lives. This is, of course, the best possible thing for each of us: to be in God's will for our lives. There is a special kind of fulfilment that can only be provided by the Lord Himself. It brings the joy that comes when we start aligning with His purpose. It also greatly reduces anxiety because rather than having to deal with the issues that come our way, we let Him have our burdens.

We cannot afford to entrust cultural transformation only to those called to full-time ministry. Imagine what could happen if lawyers, accountants, software developers, bakers, and those in every other occupation were to open their businesses to the power of the Holy Spirit. What could happen if believers decided to employ their faith to influence and impact the seven cultural mountains: business, government, media, arts and entertainment, education, family, and faith?

The old church paradigm is being renewed and refreshed. Under the old paradigm, a pastor gets a few hundred people together then ministers to them on Sunday. The people gather together, hear the Word, get right with God, then go back to their regular life Monday through Friday. This made sense back in the days when America was primarily an agricultural and rural society, because outside of family, you didn't see others all that much until you gathered together again. Before the age of radio and television, when a preacher came to town, they often had large crowds because that was the local entertainment. Once the people were there, regardless of their motives for attending, the Holy Spirit was able to work in their life.

Under this old model, the pastor needs to be a tremendous speaker, counselor, and on call 24/7 to serve the needs of the congregation. This old model is falling apart because God always had a better paradigm. In the emerging church model, each member of the congregation is called to minister to the other, not just within the family, but also within their community. The job of the full-time church worker is to equip the saints. There is no divide between holy time on Sunday and secular work during the week. Over a hundred years ago, an evangelist by the name of Bob Jones, Sr. often said, "For a Christian, there is no difference between the sacred and the secular."

Just as Jesus' garment was seamless, our lives are to be a seamless fabric with work and worship completely fluid and interwoven. On my agenda, I don't have separate lists for work and ministry tasks; all the bullet points are mixed together (not merely because I am disorganized, but because I don't differentiate between work and ministry).

> ***Then the Lord spoke to Moses, saying: "See, I have called by name Bezalel the son of Uri, the son of Hur, of the tribe of Judah. And I have filled him with the Spirit of God, in wisdom, in understanding, in knowledge, and in all manner of workmanship, to design artistic works, to work in gold, in silver, in bronze, in cutting jewels for setting, in carving wood, and to work in all manner of workmanship."*** (Exodus 31:1)

Notice this is the first instance in the Bible of someone being filled with the Spirit. Bezalel holds the chisel, but the Holy Spirit does the carving by using his hands. The work is holy because is it set apart for the Lord. Imagine being so filled with the Spirit that when you go to work, the creative force that designed the universe is able to express itself in every conference call, every board meeting, and every Excel sheet and PowerPoint presentation. Imagine doing everything you do unto the Lord and not unto men. Imagine receiving not only a paycheck for your daily needs, but an eternal reward from the Lord for your efforts. You don't have to change *what* you're doing – just *who* you are doing it for!

Observe that the Hebrew word used to describe work is *avodah*. Here are two examples:

> ***"Six days you shall work* (avodah).*"*** (Exodus 34:21)

> ***"Then man goes out to his work* (avodah), *to his labor until evening."*** (Psalm 104:23)

Now, amazingly, you will see that the very same Hebrew word *avodah* is used to describe worship, as in these examples:

> ***"This is what the Lord says: 'Let my people go, so that they may worship* (avodah) *me.'"*** (Exodus 8:1)

> ***"But as for me and my household, we will serve* (avodah) *the Lord."*** (Joshua 24:15)

The word avodah is used in the Old Testament, as you can see clearly in the above examples, to for both daily work as well as worship. What a liberating thought: let the barista make lattes as a spiritual act of worship! Whatever you do, do it for the Lord.

> ***Servants, do what you're told by your earthly masters. And don't just do the minimum that will get you by. Do your best. Work from the heart for your real Master, for God, confident that you'll get paid in full when you come into your inheritance. Keep in mind always that the ultimate Master you're serving is Christ. The sullen servant who does shoddy work will be held responsible. Being a follower of Jesus doesn't cover up bad work.*** (Colossians 3:22-25, The Message)

Our work is a holy act of worship if we set it apart for the Lord. Everything we do is honoring the Lord, if we commit it to Him. Many are under the mistaken impression that work is part of the curse placed on man after the fall. They base this on the following verses.

> ***To Adam he said, "Because you listened to what your wife said and ate from the tree about which I gave you the order, 'You are not to eat from it,' the ground is cursed on your account; you will work hard to eat from it as long as you live. It will produce thorns and thistles for you, and you will eat field plants. You will eat bread by the sweat of your forehead till you return to the ground—for you were taken out of it: you are dust, and you will return to dust."*** (Genesis 3:17-19 CJB)

However, notice what was cursed was the ground. Work itself predates the fall. Before the fall, it was easy for Adam to take care of the garden, for there were no thorns or thistles.

> ***"Adonai, God, took the person and put him in the garden of 'Eden to cultivate and care for it."*** (Genesis 2:15 CJB)

As we can see, work has nothing to do with the fall; it is part of man's original purpose. The result of the fall, in the context of work, is that it went from being a joy to a burden. It was degraded from an engaging enterprise connected with our purpose, to mere manual toil. Clearly, we can differentiate between work as in Michelangelo working on a painting, or my working on this book, from a life of subsistence, just scraping by. Jesus Christ redeemed even our work with His own perfect work at Calvary; receive your promotion now by grace through faith.

God has placed each of us into unique circumstances where we are able to impact people that no one else can reach. Many times, I will have an opportunity to speak to someone I work with about my faith or to pray for them. There are people I am able to reach that no pastor or evangelist can get to, especially because I have built up relationships of trust with them. Also, when it comes to the lost, they have a certain expectation that pastors and evangelists are somehow biased, so they have their own preconceived notions when those individuals talk with them. In their minds, when "one of their own kind" talks with them, it can be more impactful. When you walk in integrity, people will welcome you to speak into their life.

KINGDOM ENTREPRENEURSHIP

> *"Success is going from failure to failure without loss of enthusiasm."*
>
> -Winston Churchill

Risk is an important aspect of manifesting faith in business. Most successful entrepreneurs will experience failure several times before they achieve a breakthrough. It has been said, "Show me a person who never fails, and I will show you a person who never tries anything." No one is born an expert in any particular field. The greatest athlete had a time when he stumbled and was not good. The best financial manager had a time when he could not do simple addition.

Trials and risk-taking are a vital part of success, and dare I say you cannot achieve success without them. One could even argue that failures are more important to growth than success. When you make a mistake, you become aware of what you did wrong, and therefore know what not to do in the future.

It was said Thomas Edison had a pile of failed light bulb attempts that reached up to his window. Someone asked if this discouraged him, and he said, "No, for I now know hundreds of ways not make a light bulb."

On the other hand, easy success can be deceptive because many times we fail to pay attention to those specific actions that brought about success.

NEVER GIVE UP

One of the best examples of persistence is that of Abraham Lincoln. If you want to learn about somebody who didn't quit, look no further.

Born into poverty, Lincoln was faced with defeat throughout his life. He lost eight elections, failed twice in business and suffered a nervous breakdown. He could have quit many times, but he didn't, and because he didn't quit, he became one of the greatest presidents in the history of the United States.
Here is a sketch of Lincoln's road to the White House:

1816: His family was forced out of their home. He had to work to support them.

1818: His mother died.

1831: Failed in business.

1832: Ran for state legislature; lost.

1832: Also lost his job; wanted to go to law school, but couldn't get in.

1833: Borrowed some money from a friend to begin a business and by the end of the year, he was bankrupt. He spent the next seventeen years of his life paying off this debt.

1834: Ran for state legislature again; won.

1835: Was engaged to be married; sweetheart died and his heart was broken.

1836: Had a total nervous breakdown and was in bed for six months.

1838: Sought to become speaker of the state legislature; defeated.

1840: Sought to become elector; defeated.

1843: Ran for Congress; lost.

1846: Ran for Congress again; won; went to Washington and did a good job.

1848: Ran for re-election to Congress; lost.

1849: Sought the job of land officer in his home state; rejected.

1854: Ran for Senate of the United States; lost.

1856: Sought the Vice Presidential nomination at his party's national convention; received less than 100 votes.

1858: Ran for US Senate again; lost.

1860: Elected President of the United States.

Knowing our purpose helps us to persevere in such trials. If our goal is merely making money, most of us will not have the persistence to stick through failure while pursuing a new venture.

Most people prefer the status quo, even if they are not fulfilled. There is an innate risk aversion that prevents most people from living an entrepreneurial lifestyle. What people hate the most is unpredictability. In entrepreneurship, the only predictable thing is failure. Statistically speaking, most startups fail. I don't believe those numbers change much when the founder is a person of faith. The difference with Kingdom entrepreneurs is not that their startups will have a higher survival rate, but even their failures are working for them and can be turned into success.

> ***"And we know that all things work together for good to those who love God, to those who are the called according to His purpose."*** (Romans 8:28)

When we start a new project or business venture and it fails, that's not a true failure because the only true failure in the Kingdom would be to do nothing. If we build a startup and it fails, God is making that failure work for our good. Many times this adversity is building godly character. Even if we walk through the valley of the shadow of death, goodness and mercy are sure to follow. The point is to walk through it, not camp out there. Such adversity normally lasts only for a season.

An evangelist named Lester Roloff preached a sermon titled, "It Came to Pass." He pointed out all the times in the Bible where that phrase was used, and thereby encouraged people to keep fighting and enduring. He knew what he was talking about. Back in the 1970s, he had a series of homes to help incorrigible youth. His success rate was so high that it rivaled the success rate of the state-run juvenile correctional facilities of Texas where he was located. As a result, the legislature tried to shut down his homes because the treatment program was based on the Bible. He was forced to go to court many times, and even went to jail. His persistence is paying dividends still today. While Roloff passed away years ago, his homes live on, still helping troubled teenagers today.

> *"A test of a Christian's character is what he does after he comes to the blockade in the road and*

> *what his attitude is after everything has left him except Jesus. You will never know down here that Christ is all you need until Christ is all you have left."* - Lester Roloff

Stepping out in faith means taking risks. When we share the good news and stand up for our values, there is a risk of rejection. When we allocate funds to a new business, there is risk of loss. The way of the Kingdom is not to eliminate risk, but to make well thought-out and Spirit-led decisions. This means praying and asking the Holy Spirit for direction in everything we do. Many times, I have walked into a meeting, praying quietly under my breath: "Holy Spirit, let's do this together!"

When you do this, it is amazing to see what God can do. To be sure, there will be moments of apparent failure. The Bible says, ***"Yes, and all who desire to live godly in Christ Jesus will suffer persecution."*** (2 Timothy 3:12) However, there are many times when God will do great things.

BRING SABBATH POWER INTO WORK

One of the most powerful things we can do in our work is to rest.

Yes, you read that correctly. In today's culture of ubiquitous connectivity, resting is extremely difficult to do. If we cannot rest, the diagnosis is simple: we have not truly trusted God. I realize in many circles, both secular and spiritual, when I talk about the importance of rest, this statement almost borders on "heresy."

Today's western culture places a high premium on busyness. This should be differentiated from hard work. My parents are hard workers and they instilled that value in me, but that's not what I am talking about. I am talking about a heart attitude of rest and trust as opposed to the busyness of the world, which is often a façade. The alternative definition of busyness is "lively but meaningless activity." Modern people are constantly projecting an air of busyness because it validates us as important people. After all, people who aren't busy aren't important, right?

This idea that busyness is a sign of character is a lie that has crept into the collective culture over the past generation and has been amplified by technology. This was predicted in the book of Daniel. ***"But you, Daniel, shut up the words, and seal the book until the time of the end; many shall run to and fro, and knowledge shall increase."*** (Daniel 12:4) Doesn't this sound like our modern generation where people are busier with things even outside of work and spend most of the time on their cell phones or surfing the Internet?

Just a few generations ago, success was often defined by the amount of leisure time a person was able to enjoy. Those who had "made it" might spend a month in Cote D'Azur. Nowadays, it's hard for many to imagine taking a month off every year. Truth be told, most of us are responding to emails seven days a week.

If we commit our work-life to the Lord, it liberates us. Yes, I work hard and do my best to serve my clients and partners when I am "on the clock," but ultimately, I trust the Lord to take care of everything. When I am at work, I work as hard as I can, giving it my all; it has all my attention and I try not to focus on anything else. However, the reverse is also true: when I am off work, my time is devoted to my family and I do not mingle work with my home life unless absolutely necessary. This enables me to have a proper balance of family time, rest and work. No matter what I am doing, I want to cultivate and radiate an attitude of rest and faith. That means maintaining a calm demeanor even when challenges arise. And it is quite a testimony when crisis strikes but you remain calm and in faith.

The principle of sabbatical rest is built into creation. For six days, God created the heavens and the earth. On the pinnacle of the sixth day, he created man. Now that his crown jewel was created, he could rest on the following day – the seventh day. Mankind was created and born into the Sabbath. We were made to enjoy God's perfect and finished work all the time! That is why our calendar is based on a week with seven days in it.

Notice that all the cultures around the world have the seven-day week. During the French Revolution, the secular government instituted a ten-day week to get away from the Judeo-Christian heritage. The "calendrier révolutionnaire français" was implemented from 1793 to 1805. They were unable to change the length of the week. To this day, the seven-day week stands and, in fact, all of history is recorded and divided by a single moment: before and after Christ.

God instituted the principle of Sabbath in order for His people to proactively trust Him for provision. It takes faith to not work! God can do much more with six days of work than we can with seven days. The Sabbath is meant for our good. We need down time to recharge physically, emotionally, spiritually and to have a special family time.

An impressive corporate example is that of Chick-fil-A, which is a US based chicken restaurant franchise founded by Truett Cathy in 1964. All the restaurants are closed on Sunday. Chick-fil-A, however, makes five times more money than other chicken fast food franchises. In short, they are crushing the competition while working less! According to their corporate website:

> Our founder, Truett Cathy, made the decision to close on Sundays in 1946 when he opened his first restaurant in Hapeville, Georgia. Having worked seven days a week in restaurants open twenty-four hours, Truett saw the importance of closing on Sundays so that he and his employees could set aside one day to rest and worship if they choose–a practice we uphold today.

MANAGEMENT DELEGATION

When Moses led God's people out of Egypt, he initially took a huge burden on his shoulders. He sat judging all the disputes that arose within Israel from the greatest to the smallest. It was exhausting, non-stop work. When his father-in-law, Jethro, the priest of Midian, came to visit, he observed all this and said: ***"What is this thing that you are doing for the people? Why do you alone sit, and all the people stand before you from morning until evening?"*** (Exodus 18:14)

Moses was wise enough to take his father-in-law's advice, following which he recruited from the twelve tribes of Israel, training them in the law and delegating the work to them. This is a key principle for Kingdom entrepreneurs and is vital in any successful organization. In the startup stage of a business, the founder typically does everything including sales, marketing, product development, operations and administration. As his business matures, an astute manager is humble enough to delegate activities to maximize productivity. If this is not done, the manager will become the bottleneck in the business operations.

There are several reasons a manager may resist this longer than they should. One of the reasons is the fear of a loss of prestige. When you are doing all the responsibilities, everyone needs you and is dependent on you. By delegating, those under you have a tendency to go to those you have delegated authority in a certain area. They will also come to admire and look up to this person when they used to come to you. This can be a source of pride, causing you to be reluctant to give it up.

The main principle I intend to highlight by referring to sabbatical rest and management delegation is: less is more. The logic of the world says if you work harder, you will get more results. Yet, when we trust God and put Him first in everything, including our work life, then His supernatural provision enables us to be more efficient.

Tim Ferriss brings out this principle nicely in his book, *The 4 Hour Workweek.* The end analysis is simple: less is more.

"The blind quest for cash is a fool's errand … if you can free your time and location, your money is automatically worth three to ten times as much."

Ultimately, Kingdom entrepreneurs are not working for money; they make money work for them. These leaders in the marketplace are able to trust God for provision (as discussed in the principle of Sabbath) and delegate authority and responsibility to others. No one in Israel was as experienced or qualified as Moses to preside as a judge. However, going to Moses for every little task would not have been the best use of his time. Rather, Moses empowered others to step into positions of leadership to serve the needs of the people. We each have to first consider our talents and abilities, and then focus on the most important priorities.

Another Scriptural example of this principle of delegation occurs in Acts 6. A dispute had arisen over the distribution of food. The disciples took immediate and decisive action to resolve the conflict by delegating the authority and responsibility for this task.

> ***It is not desirable that we should leave the word of God and serve tables. Therefore, brethren, seek out from among you seven men of good reputation, full of the Holy Spirit and wisdom, whom we may appoint over this business; but we will give ourselves continually to prayer and to the ministry of the word.*** (Acts 6:2)

What happened was the apostles acted wisely by delegating this work, which led to the challenge being fully resolved while enabling the apostles to focus on their core work. In my investment management business, I fully delegate the portfolio management, trading and execution, research and development, fund administration, operations, and other tasks. This allows me to devote all my time and energy to focusing on the corporate strategy, key client relationships and overall management. Most bright-eyed MBAs would attribute the concept of division of labor to Adam Smith's *Wealth of Nations*, but we see this principle has a precedent nearly 3,000 years earlier in Scripture.

One can overlay the Pareto principle, which many know of as the "80/20" rule, to delegate tasks in the most efficient way. The Pareto principle is an interesting phenomenon that can be observed in just about any data set. In 1906, Italian economist Vilfredo Pareto noted eighty percent of Italy's land was owned by twenty percent of the people. He then observed his herb garden and noticed twenty percent of the pea plants produced eighty percent of the peas. Other general examples include twenty percent of taxpayer's supply eighty percent of a nation's revenue; twenty percent of roads support eighty percent of traffic; twenty percent of the team completes eighty percent of the work; twenty percent of customers account for eighty percent of the revenue or complaints. In short, the Kingdom entrepreneur must find his twenty percent and focus on it, delegating the rest of the work to others. Think of it this way: what small things can I do, in a short amount of time, with little money, which will have the biggest impact?

Our quest is to identify those activities that are extremely profitable and leveraged in order to have the maximum amount of positive impact in the world. For instance, our housekeeper does an excellent job ironing shirts. She can probably iron five dress shirts in the time it takes me to iron one. Perhaps if I practiced and worked at it, I could do a bit better. But why would I? She's much better at it, it blesses me, and she is well-compensated for the work. It frees me to focus on the gifts and talents God has given me.

We can take this concept to another level by squaring the data set. For example, if twenty percent of my clients represent eighty percent of my income, what happens if we apply the Pareto principle to the selected twenty percent group of clients? If we analyze twenty percent of the top twenty percent, that is to say four percent of the overall client base, we will observe only four percent of clients account for sixty-four percent of the income.

I had a phone call with my most important prospective client this month for a grand total of thirty minutes. That thirty-minute phone call will produce more revenue for my business than all the other calls and meetings I had in the entire month. Finding only one more client like him would be more efficient than adding 100 other clients.

REPLACE YOURSELF

Kingdom entrepreneurs surround themselves with the best talent possible. This was one of the keys to success of President Ronald Reagan. He knew he wasn't an expert in every area, so he picked people who were the best in their fields and placed them in his cabinet. Then he mostly left them alone to run their departments as they saw fit. As a result, America went from a time of high interest rates, high unemployment and high inflation to a time when each of these issues dramatically improved. Under his administration, revenues to the government doubled and the GDP grew almost five percent. It is also noteworthy that Reagan was known as being a strong evangelical Christian.

Worldly managers, however, build teams with inferior talent and control structures intended to protect their power and prestige. For Kingdom entrepreneurs, prestige as well the opinion of others is altogether irrelevant. We are performing for an audience of One.

In Numbers 27, Moses is told by God that he will die like his older brother, Aaron, not being allowed to enter the Promised Land (explained in verse 14). How does Moses respond? Does he try to change God's mind or complain about His judgment? No. Moses thinks not of himself but of the others. With the true heart of a shepherd, Moses' first reaction is to ask the Lord to appoint a man as head of Israel to replace him, so that the people of Israel may not end up as sheep without a shepherd.

Thus, God assigns Joshua, who possesses the Spirit, to this task (verse 18).

Good managers are always looking to replace themselves rather than building self-dependent structures. Indeed, one of the greatest keys to success is whether you are able to replicate yourself in other people. There have been many great men and women who ran great organizations, but because they were not able to find proper successors, after they moved on, their ministries and companies went down to where they are today: a pale shadow of their former glory.

Even Moses was replaceable. True Kingdom entrepreneurs are always thinking of empowering others. The Bible records in 2 Chronicles 22:5 that King David made preparations for the kingdom to succeed after his death: ***"So David prepared abundantly before his death."*** Let's think beyond ourselves and consider how we can empower others with God's help.

Prayer: *Heavenly Father, I pray for a courageous and pioneering spirit, that I may be a Kingdom entrepreneur. Show me how the truths mentioned above apply to my life specifically. I declare that everything I do, I do it for you, my Lord and my God. From now on, I recognize my daily work as an act of worship to you. In your mercy, help me to delight in your will and walk in your way, to the glory of your holy name. Amen.*

Meditation III

Prayer: Relationship with the Father

"Lord, teach us to pray." (Luke 11:1)

Prayer bridges the gap between what should be and what is. Turn your worries into prayers of faith. Watchman Nee gave a beautiful analogy: our prayer lays down spiritual train tracks. God's power is the locomotive engine. The locomotive doesn't go anywhere tracks have not been laid. Our burden in prayer is to lay the tracks in every area for God's power to roll through.

> ***"Be anxious for nothing, but in everything by prayer and supplication, with thanksgiving, let your requests be made known to God; and the peace of God, which surpasses all understanding, will guard your hearts and minds through Christ Jesus."*** (Philippians 4:6-7)

Probably the most important thing in my work is to pray. Prayer is the highest part of our calling. In it, we become more and more like Jesus who ever lives to make intercession for us. Prayer is a sacred duty entrusted to us; it is work from which the grace for all other work is supplied. We are called, like righteous Elijah, to pray the prayer of faith, which avails much.

It takes a courageous heart to believe what mighty influence our prayers can have. Sometimes I ride my mountain bike up into the woods and just pray. Normally that quiet time is more productive than eight hours sitting at a computer screen in terms of strategic thinking. I find one strategic idea can have a much greater impact than many hours of busywork. If I compare my resources to the technological infrastructure, financial and human capital available to some of my competitors in London and New York, I am vastly outgunned. Meanwhile, thousands of investment management firms are closing and/or consolidating every year. The bureaucracy, regulatory burdens, and legal costs associated with running a financial business have never been higher and are second in complexity only to the nuclear industry. All these costs typically flow downstream to end investors, teachers, doctors, carpenters—all of whom are oblivious to what's going on in their pension funds. The fact that this huge increase of financial regulation has scarcely benefited the main street investor or made anyone safer is beyond the scope of this book. The point is this: I can't afford not to pray. As Martin Luther said "I have so much to do that I shall spend the first three hours in prayer." If I am able to stand in the marketplace, then I stand only by His grace.

Lord, teach us to pray. Yes, this is our great need. We all know the saying, "if you give a hungry man a fish, you feed him for a day, but if you teach him how to fish, you feed him for a lifetime." We are distracted by so many temporary needs and desires, fish for a day. Prayer is the fishing pole and we need the master to teach us how to use it. Today, it may be, "Lord, teach me to be a good husband" and tomorrow, "Lord, teach me how to make wealth," but underlying all temporal need is the most imperative lesson for the blessed life: "Lord, teach me to pray." This is where we connect with the unseen realm and have fellowship with the Most High God.

The faculty of the great business schools are filled with tenured professors who are professional academics and never ran a business in their lives. Not so with our teacher Jesus. He teaches not only in word, but also in deed.

> *Nothing delights him more than to find those whom He can take with Him into the Father's presence, whom he can clothe with power to*

> *pray down God's blessing on those around them, whom He can train to be His fellow workers in the intercession by which the kingdom is to be revealed on earth.*[3]

Just as the high priest Aaron stood between Israel and the outbreak of plague, so too are we are called to stand in the gap. If we withdraw from the marketplace, we will never have the heart of an intercessor. Prayer is not getting God to go along with our plans. It's more about seeking Him, finding out His desires, praying those out and seeing them come to pass. Instead of trying to get God to bless what you are doing, find out what He is doing and get on His bandwagon.

Prayer is not merely supplication, bringing a wish list before God. No, the purest and highest form of prayer is revealed in Psalm 100:4: ***"Enter into His gates with thanksgiving, and into His courts with praise. Be thankful to Him, and bless His name."***

Notice the progression: entering through the gates with thanksgiving and, again, another level of intimacy, closer to the *skekinah* glory comes with praise. A useful acronym for the progression of prayer is ACTS:

Adoration: Give God praise and honor for who He is as Lord over all.

Confession: Honestly deal with the sin in your life.

Thanksgiving: Express what you're grateful for in your life and in the world around you.

Supplication: Pray for the needs of others and yourself.

---

[3] Andrew Murray, With Christ in the School of Prayer

When faced with overwhelming odds from a superior military force, rather than surrendering and suing for peace, Jehoshaphat sent forth the worshippers, and the battle was won, though not by might but by praise. If you suddenly find yourself facing massive opposition, start praising God with all your strength. When you do this, it accomplishes several things. First, it declares publicly that you are trusting in and loving God, not just for all the good things and times, but because of who He is, not what He does. This is what Job did in the midst of his trials that were more extensive than anything we will probably have to endure. He declared, ***"though he slay me, yet will I trust in him."*** (Job 13:15) This was a powerful shout-out to God that let the devil know he had lost his wager with God.

Even Jesus noted the importance of praise, citing it as a source of strength when he said, ***"Out of the mouth of babes and nursing infants, you have perfected praise."*** (Matthew 21:16) So was Jesus misquoting Scripture when He said this? Of course, he was referring to Psalm 8:2, which states: ***Out of the mouth of babes and nursing infants, you have ordained strength.*** No, the Lord is merely expounding on the truth found in the Tanakh, for our benefit, that we can see the correlation between praise and strength. The joy of the Lord is our strength. As we focus on Him, enjoy Him, and rejoice in what He is doing, things will move in the spiritual realm.

So if nothing else, let your prayers be saturated with praise. For a marvelous example of this in the New Testament, consider the case of Paul and Silas. They were in the city of Philippi and had just led a wealthy woman to the Lord. She invited them to come and live in her house while they preached the gospel to the people in the city. One day, while they were preaching, a young girl who was possessed with a spirit of divination mocked them during the service. Realizing this was a distraction and had the potential to hinder the preaching of the gospel, Paul cast out the evil spirit.

Men of the city who used this young girl to make them money were upset at the loss of their livelihood, so they called the authorities who beat Paul and Silas and put them in prison. They were not just put into a cell; their hands and feet were put in chains against the wall so they could not move. It would have been easy to become discouraged, thinking, "Here we were just trying to do right and obey God. Why is this happening to us? When Peter was put in jail, an angel was sent to get him out. Where is our angel?"

However, at midnight they decided there was no sense in having a pity party over what happened, so they began to sing praises to God. The Bible says in Acts 16:26 that suddenly an earthquake shook the city and opened up all the prison doors. Rather than escaping, Paul and Silas remained in their cell, worshipping God. When the guard came, he thought everyone had escaped and knew his superiors would have him executed for it. However, Paul reassured him they were all still here and as a result, this man and his entire family were saved. All because of praise.

Praise is also the best testimony to the world that what you have is genuine. Many times during the Roman persecutions, Christians were in the arena and when the lions were released, they shouted for joy and praised God that they were counted worthy to suffer for Him. Spectators in the stands, who moments before had delighted at the thought of seeing blood, became overwhelmed by their attitude and said, "I want what they have."

Even today, when Christians face martyrdom, they often provide a conviction to their murderers that unnerves them and has resulted in some of them becoming Christians themselves. The world is used to people selling out, so when you praise God even when all seems lost, it is the greatest testimony you can give, and provides the Holy Spirit with an amazing ability to work. What am I saying? Simply this: saturate your prayers with praise. Even if you have no idea what to say, just praise God regardless of the circumstances. As you do this, faith is released. It's not the quality of the words, it's the faith behind them for ***without faith it is impossible to please Him, for he***

who comes to God must believe that He is, and that He is a rewarder of those who diligently seek Him. (Hebrews 11:6)

Make it your practice to praise God, no matter what. As soon as I get some bad news or a negative experience, my reflex is to immediately speak out: ***"I will bless the Lord at all times, His praise shall continually be in my mouth."*** (Psalm 34:1) How many times I have said that verse through clenched teeth with tears streaming down my face! And it really blesses the Lord. He likes it when you pray. According to Proverbs 15:8, ***the prayer of the upright is His delight***. I believe He treasures these moments; not that we are in deep pain, but that even in our pain, we would speak out our faith and trust in Him, who alone is faithful and trustworthy. The opportunity to praise God through trying circumstances is unique to this side of eternity.

Prayer: *Father, I recognize my prayer life is not what it should be. I do not know how to pray as I ought to. Perhaps I have been overly focused on my own needs and wants, but I resolve to praise you at all times and in all circumstances. In your grace, enable me to live a life of ceaseless prayer by the power of your Holy Spirit that my prayer life would be powerful and effective in the establishment of your will, on earth as it is in heaven. Amen.*

Meditation IV

Sonship: Your Royal Identity

"And if children, then heirs – heirs of God and joint heirs with Christ…" (Romans 8:17)

If you have made Jesus Christ the Lord of your life and believed in Him for salvation, then the Bible says you are a co-heir with Him. In fact, you are a son or daughter of the Most High God and are entitled to a royal inheritance that goes beyond just being part of the royal family. This revelation is so stunning, so paradigm shattering that if it wasn't so clearly explained in the Scriptures, it would be hard to believe.

Knowing our identity as prince or princess in the Kingdom of Heaven changes everything. With this revelation, we begin to derive our identity and self-worth from who we are rather than what we do. In a world of uncertainty, we place our hope in the one who never changes. Our confidence comes from what He has said about us: that we are children of God. People may come against you, circumstances may be contrary, you may even be disappointed in yourself, but you take heart in the fact that you are in God's family, which is irrevocable. Receiving a deep revelation of your identity in Christ is the key to having the boldness and courage to face any challenge.

One does not earn an inheritance, it is simply received. The competitive landscape of Wall Street is the exact opposite, being clearly performance-based. The cliché is, "You are only as good as your last trade." This is the mentality that pervades today's financial markets and exacerbates our fear and greed. The implication is that you can perform well for years, even decades, but there is no forgiveness for a momentary slump. One can never satisfy the idols of career, money, and success. These false gods always demand more. The intensity and pressure of the Wall Street ethos can easily lead one to compromise one's values. Some think the ends always justify the means, but that's not the wisdom of the Kingdom. We are called to trust God, even if His way "costs us." A righteous man swears to his own hurt and doesn't change! (Psalm 15:4)

The good news about being in God's Kingdom is that being a member is not performance-based, because your elder brother took care of all that when He paid the price for your sins at Calvary. Salvation is not something you can lose any more than you can cease being a member of your earthly family.

That being said, a faithful interpretation of the Scriptures would show that performance is important to God. There are things you can do to increase or decrease your inheritance, which is something apart from being placed into the royal family at salvation. The good news is that since God has an infinite treasury and all power is given to Him, you are not in competition with anybody. In fact, Paul tells us in 2 Corinthians 10:12 that we are not to compare our performance to that of someone else. Our rewards in heaven are based on how we serve Him on earth, but God will not take something away from us because somebody did it better than us.

You may have heard the words, "*Only one life down here, twill soon be past. Only what's done for Christ will last.*" (C.T. Studd) However, I wonder how often we truly meditate on the meaning of those words.

It is important to point out that this is only relevant to a person who is a son or daughter of God. Contrary to what many religious leaders teach today, the saying, "Man is born in the image of God" is not true. What makes this statement erroneous is one single word. The correct phrase is "man **was** born in the image of God."

Without going into a lengthy theological discussion, the Bible says in Genesis 5:3 that Adam ***"begat a son in his own***

likeness." Adam was made in the image of God, but when he fell, the image was defiled. This assertion is supported by 1 Corinthians 15:49, which states: ***as we have borne the image of the man of dust, we shall also bear the image of the heavenly Man.*** Ever since the fall, every person is born in Adam's image, not God's. This is not to say you are not a special creation, but this distinction is important. Only those who are born in the image of God can meet the qualifications to be members of the royal family.

Just as is the case with earthly monarchies, it is a question of DNA. Jesus is referred to by the Apostle Paul in 1 Corinthians 15:45 as the "last Adam." If you want to be part of God's family, with all the benefits, you need to be in the bloodline of the second, or last Adam. This is what Jesus referred to as being "born again." You are born spiritually into the lineage of the second Adam when you acknowledge your sinful state and need of a Savior to pay the debt for you.

Then, when you acknowledge that Jesus paid this sin debt in your place and rose again on the third day, and trust not in any works you do or religion, but in the finished work of Jesus, and ask Him to save you, He will give you the free gift of salvation through this new birth.

Perhaps the most important question ever asked is found in Matthew 22:42 by Jesus. He said, ***"What do you think about the Christ? Whose Son is he?"***

How you answer this question will determine your family. Will you say Jesus is just a man and remain in the family of Adam, or will you acknowledge Jesus is "God manifested in the flesh" and be adopted into the royal family? Choose life!

BREAKING THE CHAINS OF ERROR

What's the hardest place in the world to reach? Perhaps the Mariana Trench at the bottom of the Pacific; over seven miles below the surface where the pressure is 1,000 times sea level? What about the summit of Everest or K2, places so high that a man cannot survive without oxygen due to the thin air? Is it Death Valley with the world's hottest temperature of 56.7 degrees Celsius (134F)? Could it be the East Antarctic Plateau, the coldest place on earth measuring -92 degrees Celsius (-133.6F)? No, the hardest place to reach is the human heart. Only the word of truth, the sword of the Spirit, can do it.

People say the truth shall set you free, citing the Bible. However, as is often the case, they do not quote the verse accurately. Jesus said in John 17:17 that the truth will only set a person free if they know the truth. The physical properties of electricity have been true since the beginning of creation and were able to be harnessed for our benefit, yet men walked in darkness for ages. The reason is having access to this amazing source of energy does no good, if you do not know how to harness it.

He who knows not the gospel of truth walks in darkness and his mind is open to deception. Jesus says: ***I am the way, the truth and the life***, not a way. The world says that truth is relative and there are many equally valid ways to salvation, heaven, nirvana, enlightenment, and all other names for the afterlife. The claim of Jesus and the claims of the world are mutually exclusive. Either Jesus is wrong or the world is wrong; it is impossible for both to be correct, no matter how hard men try to make it so. Look at the world with all of its problems, crime, and hatred. Now look at Jesus, who is love personified, God being willing to die for His creation. Whom will you believe? I think I'll stick with Jesus.

To be sure, the "many paths" fallacy does hold a certain attraction; how could it not? I mean, the idea of being able to pick your own standards for entering a place of perfection and peace; who would pass up a deal like that? Consider this: If there is any way besides the cross, then God would be a cruel monster to allow Jesus to suffer as He did. Not only that, Jesus would have been the biggest fool in the universe for volunteering to do it. If the cross was unnecessary because any other path is equally viable, then Calvary is a cosmic outrage. No, the truth is ***"no one comes to the Father, but by me."*** (John 14:6) For the most part, the world doesn't hate people who believe in God. They will even get along with people who think they need Jesus to save them, as long as that's their opinion. What the world hates is the apparent exclusivity of the gospel.

> ***"Enter by the narrow gate; for wide is the gate and broad is the way that leads to destruction, and there are many who go in by it. Because narrow is the gate and difficult is the way which leads to life, and there are few who find it."*** (Matthew 7:13-14)

This doesn't seem like it can get any more exclusive than that, but before you think this sounds elitist and discriminatory, remember the gospel is open to the whole world, to people of every race, tribe, and tongue. From the least to the greatest, from the worst to the best, every beating heart on the planet is only one short prayer away from eternal salvation.

Oh, but the hardest place to reach is the human heart. Despite the ease with which God has made it for mankind to obtain eternal life, many will spurn His offer; instead insisting on doing it their own way, essentially saying they believe they are more right on this issue than God. Only the word of truth, only the sword of the Spirit, can do it.

The Emancipation Proclamation was signed by President Abraham Lincoln on January 1, 1863. Legally speaking, the proclamation declared, "all people being held as slaves are, and henceforward shall be free." With the stroke of the pen, the institution of slavery was abolished for all time in the US. However, this legal right was not the actual experience of most slaves at the time. There were slaves being held on remote, rural plantations who continued living under the same conditions, in some cases for decades after the Emancipation Proclamation. The truth is, they were legally free, but were still held in bondage because they were kept ignorant of this truth.

The truth is only effective in so much as you know it and then take that knowledge and act on it, for Jesus said, ***"And ye shall* know *the truth, and the truth shall make you free."*** (John 8:32) How many of us are legally free, yet still live like slaves?

Today, the accuser of the brethren continues lurking about to deceive us by attempting to rob us of our legal rights and privileges as children of the light. He says, "You are a slave to sin, you can't change. You can't break out of that bad habit. Look, you don't pray enough, you don't do enough (insert religious activity). You don't do this, you don't do that. God would never want a loser like you. You are worthless. Why would a holy and pure God want someone as filthy and evil as you?"

To which we reply, "Yes, indeed, we are slaves! **Slaves to righteousness! Prisoners of hope!** Bond-servants of the only sovereign Lord and King! Hallelujah."

There is no greater freedom than knowing you are under His grace. Grace is truly humbling, for it means "unmerited favor." It means you have zero claim on deserving eternal life because of the deeds you have done. God gives it to those who know they cannot earn it on their own. This is why it can be difficult for people of some means to be saved, for the idea of obtaining something for which they have not paid for or earned is repugnant.

There is no greater confidence than knowing *it is finished.* No greater liberty than declaring: ***"As for me and my house, we shall serve the Lord."*** (Joshua 24:15) You are a victor in Christ Jesus. You are more than a conqueror, a champion. Even as I witness my little daughter, Léa, taking her first steps, our Father yearns to see His children stand up and walk forward by the Spirit.

On the topic of slavery, please take note of the Clapham group. This group of believers from eighteenth and nineteenth century England was comprised of bankers, lawyers, administrators, parliamentarians, diplomats, authors, and some clergy. In short, I would describe the Clapham group as a marketplace movement. It's an archetype for present day social activists who are committed to transforming the world on behalf of our Lord Jesus Christ. On Earth, as it is in Heaven. This remarkable group of believers succeeded in achieving, among other things, the complete abolition of slavery in the UK, starting with the passage of the Slave Trade Act of 1807. Never underestimate the impact of the Kingdom.

Forget all those things you did wrong in the past. It's covered by the cross. For those who have trusted Jesus Christ as their Savior, God has cast them behind his back (Isaiah 38:17). He has removed them as far from you as the east is from the west (Psalm 103:12). He has cast them in the depths of the deepest ocean (Micah 7:19).

Jeremiah prophesies of the New Covenant that, ***"They all shall know me, from the least of them to the greatest of them," says the Lord. "For I will forgive their iniquity, and their sin I will remember no more."*** (Jeremiah 31:34) That's a truth more powerful than all the electricity in the world. For our Lord Jesus both proclaimed and fulfilled the prophecy of Isaiah, which says: ***"The Spirit of the Lord God is upon Me, because the Lord has anointed Me to preach good tidings to the poor; He has sent Me to heal the brokenhearted, to proclaim liberty to the captives, and the opening of the prison to those who are bound."*** (Isaiah 61:1)

Forget what you did right in the past. Let your good works be like a surprise on the day of the Lord, when He comes in power and glory with His rewards for us; lest we fall into pride, for there is nothing we have which we have not been given. If we boast, let us boast in the Lord, for it is the Lord who is the strength of our lives. Amen.

Prayer: *Father, thank you that you have forgiven our iniquity and not remembered our sin. According to Psalm 32:1, "Blessed is he whose transgression is forgiven, whose sin is covered." We are greatly blessed, indeed. Thank you, Heavenly Father. We ask for a fresh revelation of this profound truth, so that we may walk by the Spirit in freedom and liberty, no* *longer captives to fear and guilt, but set free by our Lord and Savior to reign in life. Help us to break out of the mundanity of daily routines and negative thought patterns. In your grace, Father, renew our minds by the washing of the Word so that we may think pure, good thoughts and share wholesome, uplifting words to those you bring across our paths today. Amen.*

Meditation V

Grace: Reign of the Spirit

"All things are possible to him who believes." (Mark 9:23)

"Ye shall know the truth, and the truth shall make you free." (John 8:32)

"According to your faith let it be to you." (Matthew 9:29)

My toddler Samantha always wants me to pick her up and carry her. It doesn't matter if I'm carrying two bags of groceries. She gets in front of me to block my path, then holds up her hands, looking up expectantly. If I do not immediately oblige, she always persists. I believe the Spirit showed me this is how we ought to pray.

In **Prayer:**

Look up to our Papa (focus on Him).
Get close to Him.
Have childlike faith, knowing He most certainly will answer.
Persist, persist, persist: "Papa, Papa, Papa!"
In response, He will ultimately:
Lift us up unto Himself.
Intimately embrace us.
Change our perspective and vantage point, so that we see as He sees.
Ensure we effortlessly cover more ground then we ever could have on our own (supernatural grace).

When we make Jesus the Lord of our life, we enable the supernatural power of God to manifest in ourselves. So long as we insist on being the boss, we will always be limited to "sowing and reaping" in the natural realm according to our ability rather than reaping heavenly blessings.

If Jesus is the boss of my life, He has assumed all my problems as well. It has been said that in every Christian's heart is a throne and a cross. At any given time, you and Jesus are on one or the other. If you are on the throne of your life, He is on the cross. If you are on the cross, then it means He is on the throne of your life.

The spirit does the heavy lifting. Though we are weak in the flesh, through the spirit we are strong. Though we were self-centered and proud, through the spirit we abound in infinite and eternal love.

I believe appropriating God's grace is the secret to alleviating the soul-crushing stress and anxiety so prevalent today. God's grace empowers us to handle any situation. When we begin walking by the Spirit and allow Jesus to be the Lord of our work-life, we are elevated from a place of reaping and sowing in our own strength to where we are now able to appropriate God's supernatural grace into our daily work. The Holy Spirit knows the answer to every problem you are facing. He wants to be your comforter and leader. He is with you in every business meeting, every conference call, the question is, are you going to allow Him to participate in the meeting or the conversation? Imagine if the creative power of the Holy Spirit were unleashed into our corporate culture. There would be wisdom for every decision, and self-discipline for risk management.

> ***". . . much more they which receive abundance of grace and of the gift of righteousness shall reign in life by one, Jesus Christ."*** (Romans 5:17)

Oh, what a Scripture to lay hold of! As His life reigns in us, we shall reign in life. It's not a passive thing. We must continually receive this abundance of grace and this gift of righteousness. If "reigning in life" is the last phrase you would use to describe yourself, then this is a word for you. Today is the day. There is not just barely enough grace at the bottom of the barrel to get you limping into heaven. No, there is a super abundance of grace you have access to, everything you need to *reign*. Believe and receive, or doubt and do without.

Here is the good news: your overdraft account is not merely brought to a zero balance; it's overflowing. The price Jesus paid is far greater than any negative balance you could possibly accrue. His blood is more than enough. There is an overflow of grace, gifts of the Spirit, and fruit of the Spirit. A seed is planted: the word of God. One little seed, but it generates new life, year after year, and if you wait long enough, you will see the flourishing orchard that has grown up from that single seed. An ever-increasing harvest.

In recent months I was exceedingly busy: making a strategic investment, reviewing financial statements, attending board meetings, plus all the regular things that come with running an investment management business while having two little babies at home that need my love and affection. I asked the Lord what to do. He said: "spend more time praying and less time in the things of the world." This is so counterintuitive and antithetical to the advice we would receive from the best-intentioned colleagues in the world. Yet, it is exactly what I needed to hear.

We are God's inheritance. He yearns to enjoy us and to have fellowship with us now. When we get in the secret place of the Most High, where we are totally vulnerable and honest, His supernatural grace will surely flow through us. Don't let anything rob you of your intimacy with the Lord. Seek Him, seek the Kingdom and His righteousness and all these things will be added unto you.

I'm the righteousness of God in Christ Jesus (2 Corinthians 5:21). Can you look in the mirror and say that? If not, perhaps you esteem your guilt and shame to be greater than the Messiah's atonement.

The woman caught in the act of adultery (John 8) discovered that grace: "neither do I condemn you." And only then, does Jesus say: "go and sin no more." Grace enables. Grace empowers. The Lord, in His kindness and mercy, takes away every accusation, all guilt and shame.

In the world, we do, do, do, and then expect to receive because we have earned it. In the workplace, in performance-based relationships, in religion in the negative sense. Yet, the gospel of grace is to be received by faith! What a joy! How light the burden. In the world, we have victory when we fight. In the Kingdom, we have victory when we surrender.

> ***For by grace you have been saved through faith, and that not of yourselves; it is the gift of God, not of works, lest anyone should boast. For we are His workmanship, created in Christ Jesus for good works, which God prepared beforehand that we should walk in them.*** (Ephesians 2:9-10)

> *"In my hand no price I bring, simply to thy cross I cling."* (Song, Rock of Ages)

Paul testifies of this in his own life: for the grace given to him was not in vain, but he labored more abundantly than them all. If you look at Paul's life before his salvation, if there is anyone who could have been saved by works, it would have been Paul. Yet, he said all the righteous things he did, he counts them as dung compared to the righteousness of Jesus Christ (Philippians 3:8).

We never get over our problems by focusing on them. Believers are always going around confessing how anxious they are, how burdened they are, how tough the conditions are these days, how much they are suffering, while putting pious little addendums on their gripes and complaints, like "but the Lord's still on the throne." Stop it! Focus instead on the Lord Jesus, who reigns supreme and is coming in power and glory. Confess the super-abundance of His grace; proclaim the gift of righteousness you continuously receive. The robe of righteousness. You don't just receive it; you keep it white and put it on every day.

Only believe. From this marvelous faith flows wholesome, empowering words and good deeds. Don't stress about it; God prepared these good works in advance that we should walk in them. *Only believe*. *Only* seek His face. Your good works by faith will be as natural as a cherry tree bearing cherries each summer. Have you seen a tree struggle to produce fruit? No, it is just something that happens every year.

Notice our Lord Jesus at the time when He came up out of the waters of baptism, and the Father said: ***"This is My beloved Son, in whom I am well pleased."*** (Matthew 3:17) These words were spoken before Jesus did any ministry, healing, or miracles. The basis of the Father's pleasure is a *relationship* with the Son; it is not based on performance. This word from the Father is the bread of sustenance which Jesus needed to withstand temptation. Again, the pattern: first *receive* love, grace, benediction, and blessing. Then, go and do.

When we come out of the waters of baptism, leaving all sin behind, the Father proclaims His unconditional love for us. You are *beloved* of the Father. You are now clothed in His righteousness.

However, this does not mean God is like some old grandfather who chuckles and overlooks sins against his word. The Bible records a situation in 2 Samuel that should give us all pause. The Ark of the Covenant had been residing in the field of an Israelite named Joshua (no relation to the Joshua who was with Moses), following its being captured by the Philistines. It had been there for many years, going back to before Saul was the king. King David decided to retrieve the Ark and bring it to Jerusalem.

> ***So they set the ark of God on a new cart, and brought it out of the house of Abinadab, which was on the hill; and Uzzah and Ahio, the sons of Abinadab, drove the new cart. And they brought it out of the house of Abinadab, which was on the hill, accompanying the ark of God; and Ahio went before the ark. Then David and all the house of Israel played music before the Lord on all kinds of instruments of fir wood, on harps, on stringed instruments, on tambourines, on sistrums, and on cymbals.***
>
> ***And when they came to Nachon's threshing floor, Uzzah put out his hand to the ark of God and took hold of it, for the oxen stumbled. Then the anger of the Lord was aroused against Uzzah, and God struck him there for his error; and he died there by the ark of God. And David became angry because of the Lord's outbreak against Uzzah; and he called the name of the place Perez Uzzah to this day. David was afraid of the Lord that day; and he said, "How can the ark of the Lord come to me?" So David would not move the ark of the Lord with him into the City of David; but David took it aside into the house of Obed-Edom the Gittite.***
> (2 Samuel 6:3-10)

A person reading this passage might think how unfair this was. Uzzah was trying to prevent the Ark from falling off the cart and being damaged. If it fell off, possibly the table of the Ten Commandments, along with the pot of manna and Aaron's rod that budded almonds might fall out on the ground and who knows what would happen. Weren't they doing a good thing taking the Ark from being outside in a dirty old field and wanting to put it in a nice clean place?

Their goals were commendable, but what they failed to remember was God wants all things to be done decently and in order (1 Corinthians 14:40). This means it is not enough to have a good motive, what we do must be done God's way if we want Him to be pleased. They should have consulted God's word on the matter before doing anything. When you go back to Genesis 3:6, look at what went through Eve's mind before she took the forbidden fruit. ***"So when the woman saw that the tree was good for food, that it was pleasant to the eyes, and a tree desirable to make one wise, she took of its fruit and did eat. She also gave to her husband with her, and he ate."*** What was wrong with her reason for wanting the fruit? Aren't those all good things to have? What's wrong with wanting to be wise? The answer is there is nothing wrong with her motives, but the entire human race was cursed because Adam and Eve went about getting these things their way rather than God's way. God told them not to do it, and that should have settled it.

When it came to moving the Ark, God made His instructions explicitly clear in writing. The first mistake was moving it on a cart pulled by oxen. Moses carefully explained how the Ark was to be carried in Numbers 4. It was to be carried by Levites using a system of rings and poles. The next mistake was for Uzzah to reach out and touch the Ark, regardless of what was about to happen to it. God gave explicit instructions for the care and transportation of the Ark, with the express, written warning that "***they shall not touch any holy thing, lest they die***" (Numbers 4:15). Uzzah was a Levite and the old saying still remains true, "Ignorance of the law is no excuse." Any Levite should have been acutely aware of these instructions.

Ignorance of the law is still no excuse even under grace. As Jesus shows us, love fulfils Torah. For it is by the law that man sees the utter depravity of his own heart; it is by the law that one comprehends the utter futility of self-actualization and self-improvement. The purpose of the law is to show us God's standards of perfection, and lets us know we can never attain it, thus helping us realize our need for a Savior. Notice all Israel was worshipping and shouting and praising, just like we see happening in many churches today with their praise services and worship directors. All these things are wonderful, but they become meaningless and hollow when the Word of God is forsaken, and we attempt to do the things of God our way.

Thus, the anger of the Lord was aroused. When it says the Lord made a breach on Uzzah, the word literally means he was cleaved in two. God's anger drove David and the Levites back to Torah to find out what was expected of them. What shall we make of all this? Have God's standards changed? Has He just swept sin under the rug? By no means. When we see the severity of God's wrath, we start to appreciate just how much Jesus did for us on the cross. He drank the cup of God's wrath to the dregs.

Now, in the age of grace, the anger of the Lord is put away by the cross; praise His name forever! This marvelous gospel of grace. Rather than anger, we receive His love, an *abundance of grace* that enables us to carry the Ark rightly into our city, into the marketplace, into our homes and churches. Everywhere the Spirit leads, we march triumphant, bearing the *Shekinah* glory of God!

Then we shall sing King David's Song of Thanksgiving when the Ark arrived at Jerusalem (1 Chronicles 16:23-29):

Sing to the Lord, all the earth;
Proclaim the good news of His salvation from day to day.
Declare His glory among the nations,
His wonders among all peoples.

For the Lord is great and greatly to be praised;
He is also to be feared above all gods.
For all the gods of the peoples are idols,
But the Lord made the heavens.

Honor and majesty are before Him;
Strength and gladness are in His place.

Give to the Lord, O families of the peoples,
Give to the Lord glory and strength.
Give to the Lord the glory due His name;
Bring an offering, and come before Him.
Oh, worship the Lord in the beauty of holiness!

Prayer: *Heavenly Father, today I come boldly before your throne of grace, asking you to multiply your grace abundantly to me, so that I may reign in life to the glory of your holy name. Righteous Father, in faith, I receive your gift and put on the robes of righteousness, believing in your precious and holy Son Jesus. I pray, Lord, in my career, my family life, in everything I do, Lord, lead me by the hand, that I might walk in every good thing you've prepared for me. Amen.*

Meditation VI

Integrity: The Structure for Blessing

"The integrity of the upright will guide them, but the perversity of the unfaithful will destroy them." (Proverbs 11:3)

Picture two prosperous men, each of them a successful private banker, walking down the Bahnhofstrasse, Zurich's answer to the Champs Elysees in France or New York's Fifth Avenue. The watches they wear are a product of Switzerland. The suits are hand-tailored in Italy. Both are well educated, cultured and multilingual. These men would be considered successful by just about any worldly standard.

Yet, there is a difference between them. It's not the Brioni suit or the Rolex. The difference is in pride and humility. The proud one says to himself, *no one gave me anything. I earned everything I have*. Sound familiar? The humble man is almost a little surprised at his success and knows it is the product of his family, upbringing, and many other variables such as race, time, and location of birth that are beyond his control. Ultimately, the humble man knows he has risen to success not because of himself, but in spite of himself. Everything good in his life is by the grace of God. There is nothing wrong with having money; the problem comes when money has you. Many frequently misquote the Bible and say money is the root of all evil, but the Scripture actually says, ***"the love of money is a root of all kinds of evil."*** (1 Timothy 6:10) Money is a wonderful servant, but a terrible master.

"You may forget that you are at every moment totally dependent on God." (CS Lewis)

God wants us; we are *His* inheritance! David said multiple times in the Psalms, ***"Bless the Lord, O my soul."*** Many read over that verse, not truly meditating on the meaning. David was saying he was going to bless God, not ask God to bless him like we often say. Let me ask you a question: are you a blessing to God today? Have you ever started the day by asking the God, "Lord, is there anything I can do for you today?" God also knows our greatest need is to have Him in our life. The greatest gift God can give us is Himself!

There have been many cases of trust fund babies who have had their lives ruined by their inheritance because they did not have the maturity to handle that kind of wealth. The inheritance of our Papa is much greater than the combined wealth of the Vanderbilt's, Rockefeller's, Kennedy's, Gates, and all the other billionaire families; He doesn't want to ruin us.

Why is the trust fund baby spoiled? Being born into wealth, they have no point of reference to help them understand and appreciate what it took to produce the wealth. This cannot help but give them a warped sense of value. The inner character structure of the heart must be developed to support the "glory weight" of the blessing. That's why we are always blessed from the inside out. God looks on the heart; man looks on the external. Kingdom entrepreneurs' external things are a mere fruit of their walk with the King. It is purely secondary to the spiritual wealth they have on the inside by their fellowship with Jesus and the Father.

Our Papa knows it's better for us to go through a heart process so we can identify with what Jesus did. The Bible describes Him as a "man of sorrows." (Isaiah 53:3) That's why we die to self. That's why we surrender; so we can build the heart integrity necessary to receive everything Papa wants to give us.

God wants to bless your storehouse, but He can only do so if you have the spiritual capacity to receive it. He will never give you something that will destroy you, and money has destroyed more good people than any disease.

The storehouse is finite; the overflow is for sowing. In Solomon's time, he was so wealthy they had to build cities just for the purpose of holding all his wealth. Now, we have something even bigger: a heavenly bank account. Have you ever seen a full bank account? I've never come across a bank account that couldn't accommodate a few more zeroes. The depth and technology linked to modern financial markets has given us an astonishing ability to preserve and grow wealth. There is a tremendous amount of dead capital in the financial system. As an example, Apple has $250 billion in cash just sitting there. Microsoft has $133 billion presently in their corporate treasury. There are countless other examples. Forbes said in July 2017 that the US corporate cash pile is sitting at $1.84 trillion. Why don't these corporations invest that capital in new technology, research, and development or human capital? There could be any number of complex answers to that question, but they can all be summed up in two human emotions: greed and fear. It's time for Kingdom entrepreneurs to unlock dormant capital and put it to use, but it will take a level of integrity and courage that only Heaven itself can supply.

I believe that God really wants you to walk in a level of prosperity and blessing beyond anything you've ever experienced. Ask God today, what is standing in the way? What area of my character must be developed?

THE PROMISED SON IN THE PROMISED LAND

> *I know men; and I tell you that Jesus Christ is no mere man. Between Him and every person in the world there is no possible term of comparison. Alexander, Caesar, Charlemagne, and I have founded empires. But on what did we rest the creations of our genius? Upon force.*

> *Jesus Christ founded His empire upon love; and at this hour millions of men would die for him.* (Napoleon Bonaparte)

Yes, indeed, the greatest of these is love.

- Take love from joy and you have only hedonism.
- Take love from holiness and you have self-righteousness.
- Take love from truth and you have bitter orthodoxy.
- Take love from mission and you have conquest.
- Take love from unity and you have tyranny. (www.enduringword.com, Dan Guzik)

Jesus is no mere man. He gave up the wealth of heaven, becoming poor that we may share in His riches. He became sin with our sinfulness that we may become the righteousness of God. He laid down His life willingly, that we may be raised to life with Him. He took the curse that we may receive the blessing of Abraham by faith.

> ***Christ has redeemed us from the curse of the law, having become a curse for us (for it is written, "Cursed is everyone who hangs on a tree"), that the blessing of Abraham might come upon the Gentiles in Christ Jesus, that we might receive the promise of the Spirit through faith. … For you are all sons of God though faith in Christ Jesus. … And if you are Christ's, then you are Abraham's seed, and heirs according to the promise.*** (Galatians 3:13, 26, 29)

The above Scripture is a lens through which the Christian reads and interprets the old covenant blessings and curses. When we read the extensive curses in Deuteronomy 28, rather than feeling a tremendous sense of personal fear and dread, we can understand in a new light what Jesus truly endured on the cross. When we read the blessings in that same chapter, we come away with a sense of awe and wonder of all that the Lord purchased with His blood.

Since we are heirs to the promises of Abraham, we can cull prophetic truth from the life of his immediate heir, the promised son, Isaac: ***"Now we, brethren, as Isaac was, are children of promise."*** (Galatians 4:28) Let's take a look at Isaac, a man of integrity who saw God's promises actualized in his life.

Genesis 26 shows, in the midst of famine, Isaac began to make his way to Egypt for relief. He got as far as Gerar of the Philistines when the Lord told him to stay in the Promised Land:

> ***Then the Lord appeared to him and said: "Do not go down to Egypt; live in the land of which I shall tell you. Dwell in this land, and I will be with you and bless you; for to you and your descendants I give all these lands, and I will perform the oath which I swore to Abraham your father. And I will make your descendants multiply as the stars of heaven; I will give to your descendants all these lands; and in your seed all the nations of the earth shall be blessed."*** (Genesis 26:2-4)

ISAAC'S 100X RETURN ON INVESTMENT

Isaac was obedient to the word of the Lord. By faith, he stayed in the land of promise:

> ***Then Isaac sowed in that land, and reaped in the same year a hundredfold; and***

> ***the Lord blessed him. The man began to prosper, and continued prospering until he became very prosperous; for he had possessions of flocks and possessions of herds and a great number of servants. So the Philistines envied him.*** (Genesis 26:12-14)

Isaac sowed seed and as a result of his obedience, while the rest of the world suffered from a famine, he reaped a hundred times that same year. That is supernatural favor! Faith without works is dead. It took tremendous faith to sow the seed in the midst of a famine, trusting that the Lord would provide water.

Recently, archaeologists planted some seeds entombed with one of the pharaohs more than three thousand years ago. Amazingly, after all these millennia, the seeds grew. Isaac could have saved the seed until conditions improved. That is what most people would have done, because sowing seed in the famine, in the flesh, would be a waste of seed. Oh, but, ***"'My thoughts*** **are** ***not your thoughts, nor*** **are** ***your ways My ways,' says the Lord.'"*** (Isaiah 55:8)

When you're a prosperous cattle rancher, you need water. Lots of it, continuously. Water is not a luxury—it's an absolute necessity. In the western United States, water is a precious commodity. People in the western US purchase "shares" of water treated like any other commodity, meaning you can sell, lease, or rent it. Many times, when developers or a city want to build a new subdivision or some other project, they are required to purchase a certain number of shares to ensure the project can sustain itself and not take shares of water from others.

By faith, Isaac received the hundred-fold blessing, and only by faith could this blessing be maintained. We need a massive, continuous flow of the Holy Spirit in the walk of faith.

Abraham dug wells in the land, but they were clogged up and being filled with earth by the Philistines. Thus, Isaac's inheritance was initially denied. In faith, Isaac dug a fresh well and the water flowed. Yet, the jealous Philistines contended for it. Humbly, he did not assert his rights, but moved on further to dig again, providing us an example of perseverance and Christ-like suffering.

> ***Also Isaac's servants dug in the valley, and found a well of running water there. But the herdsmen of Gerar quarreled with Isaac's herdsmen, saying, "The water*** **is** ***ours." So he called the name of the well Esek, because they quarreled with him. Then they dug another well, and they quarreled over that*** **one** ***also. So he called its name Sitnah. And he moved from there and dug another well, and they did not quarrel over it. So he called its name Rehoboth, because he said, "For now the Lord has made room for us, and we shall be fruitful in the land."*** (Genesis 26:19-22)

> ***"It came to pass the same day that Isaac's servants came and told him about the well which they had dug, and said to him, 'We have found water.' So he called it Shebah. Therefore the name of the city is Beersheba to this day."*** (Genesis 26:32-33)

Isaac's Wells

ESEK: Quarrel

SITNAH: Enmity

REHOBOTH: Spaciousness

SHEBAH: Oath/Seven (connotes perfection)

BEERSHEBA: Well of the oath

Have the waters of your inheritance been stopped up? Do you find yourself not having any resources from your parents and grandparents? Has the work of your hands only brought thorns and thistles? If your children and grandchildren are to have an inheritance, will you have to be the first one in your family to create it? Keep standing in faith on God's righteousness and His promise to you. ***"Faithful is he that calleth you, who also will do it."*** (1 Thessalonians 5:24) God Himself will sanctify you completely, preserving your body, soul and spirit blameless until the coming of the Lord Jesus Christ. ***"He shall bring forth your righteousness as the light and your justice as the noonday."*** (Psalm 37:6)

Your every ESEK (quarrel) brings you closer to your REHOBOTH (spaciousness). God uses every SITNAH (enmity) to bring you to your SHEBAH (promise). *Rehoboth* is the blessing on the work of your hands. And *Shebah* is the oath that the Lord has promised to perform for the seed of Abraham. *Rehoboth* is good, for it is a good thing to work and see the fruit of your labor, but *Shebah* is so much better; it is to receive the inheritance for which you did not work; to take over houses you did not build, to reap from fields where you have not sown. The Lord Jesus earned your *Shebah* well at Calvary; receive it now by faith in His perfect and finished work.

We are called to be wells through which gush rivers of living water, bringing God's promise of hope to all who thirst. The world, the enemy, and the flesh—perhaps all three—have conspired to block your well of inheritance and diminish the work of your hand. We can succumb to that proud temptation of self-pity; or we can keep moving, keep digging, keep sowing, and yes, keep seeking and asking and knocking. A breakthrough is just around the corner. Although Isaac sowed and Isaac dug, He gave all the credit to God. ***"For now the Lord has made room for us, and we shall be fruitful in the land."*** (Genesis 26:22)

The ultimate breakthrough was not the miraculous 100x harvest, nor the flowing wells of *Rehoboth* or *Shebah*, but the day when his enemy Abimelech said, "*You are blessed of the Lord,*" and sought a covenant of peace with Isaac:

> ***Then Abimelech came to him from Gerar with Ahuzzath, one of his friends, and Phichol the commander of his army. And Isaac said to them, "Why have you come to me, since you hate me and have sent me away from you?"***
>
> ***But they said, "We have certainly seen that the Lord is with you. So we said, 'Let there now be an oath between us, between you and us; and let us make a covenant with you, that you will do us no harm, since we have not touched you, and since we have done nothing to you but good and have sent you away in peace. You are now the blessed of the Lord.'"***
>
> ***So he made them a feast, and they ate and drank. Then they arose early in the morning and swore an oath with one another; and Isaac sent them away, and they departed from him in peace.*** (Genesis 26:26-31)

This covenant of peace between Isaac and his enemies is a prophetic picture of the new covenant. This feast between Isaac and Abimelech prophecies the great marriage supper of the Lamb, when those who were formerly enemies will be called from the north, south, east, and west to sit down at the feast with Abraham, Isaac, and Jacob. Thank you, Jesus! Amen.

Prayer: *Father of lights, search my heart. Shine a light on every dark place. You know me better than even I know myself. Show me the aspects of my character that need to be improved, so that I can handle true wealth for the Kingdom. Teach me to be more like Jesus every day. Amen.*

Meditation VII

Kingdom: Released by Breakthrough

The Lord has broken through my enemies before me, like a breakthrough of water. (2 Samuel 5:20)

His voice was like the sound of many waters. (Revelation 1:15)

Then all the tribes of Israel came to David at Hebron and spoke, saying, "Indeed we are *your bone and your flesh. Also, in time past, when Saul was king over us, you were the one who led Israel out and brought them in; and the Lord said to you, 'You shall shepherd My people Israel, and be ruler over Israel.'" Therefore all the elders of Israel came to the king at Hebron, and King David made a covenant with them at Hebron before the Lord. And they anointed David king over Israel. David* was *thirty years old when he began to reign,* and *he reigned forty years.* (2 Samuel 5:1-4)

Patience. Perseverance. Contentment. These are the prerequisites if we hope to receive a breakthrough. David was thirty years of age when he received this third anointing. The first anointing occurred when David was a mere teenage shepherd, nearly passed over by the Prophet Samuel.

For the Lord does not see as man sees; for man looks at the outward appearance, but the Lord looks at the heart. (1 Samuel 16:7)

We are often concerned with outward things such as position, job titles, and status, but the Lord is interested in the integrity and purity of our heart. He cannot bring breakthrough to those who are corrupt in heart; for that would not be a blessing, but a curse. Just as a potter molds a lump of clay to make it into what he envisions in his mind's eye, the Lord orchestrates events in our life to develop in us something of His own character, for the ultimate purpose of being able to entrust His plans to us.

Imagine if David would have taken the throne immediately following his first anointing, before going through all the trials and tests he faced before assuming the throne. Threats from Philistines, threats from Saul, losing his temper to where he almost killed innocent people because a man named Nabal insulted him; one time even his own men were ready to stone him at Ziklag.

Yet, in all this, God prepared David to become the greatest and most celebrated king in the history of Israel, one whose throne has been established forever. If he became king at his first anointing, perhaps he would have reigned only a short time. Remember, even when he became king, there was a bloody civil war between him and the house of Saul, with people supporting both sides. It is possible that not having experience, David may have been reckless and lost his kingdom to older, more experienced warriors. There is an old saying, "fools rush in where wise men fear to tread." Because of God's Kingdom process, even though David had to persevere through many hardships, His reign was established and solid: thirteen years of resistance training versus forty years on the throne.

HUMILITY IS THE KEY TO GODLY PROMOTION

Our motive for breakthrough should never be self-promotion; though if we are humble, the Lord will lift us up in due time. No, the true and pure motive of our heart is glory for God and blessing for His people. ***"Humble yourselves therefore under the mighty hand of God that he may exalt you in due time: Casting all your care upon Him for He cares for you."*** (1 Peter 5:6-7)

This brings up an interesting question. How does one remain humble while in a secular workforce that thrives on self-aggrandizement? When you go for job interviews, some of the questions are: name three of your biggest accomplishments, why should I hire you over the other candidates, and other questions that ask you to essentially "brag" on yourself. How do you do this while obeying God's command to be humble? The answer is found in a pair of Bible verses.

The first verse is found in a statement by John the Baptist in John 3:30 where he says, speaking of Jesus, ***"He must increase, but I must decrease."*** Jesus said among those born of women, there was none greater than John the Baptist, so how could this be if John said he needed to decrease? The answer is found in Joshua 3:7 after the death of Moses and just before Joshua led the people in to conquer and claim the land which God promised Abraham centuries ago: ***"And the Lord said unto Joshua, 'This day will I begin to magnify thee in the sight of all Israel, that they may know that, as I was with Moses, so I will be with thee.'"*** (Joshua 3:7)

Notice God said He would begin to magnify Joshua's presence before the people. Here we have the biblical formula. Your job is to fulfill John 3:30 and make yourself small, by being humble and realizing whatever good things people may say about you, you know the truth, which is that it is all by the grace of God. While you might offer up a "thank you," you do not take credit for it.

When you do this, Joshua 3:7 kicks in. God will then place a spiritual magnifying glass between you and those around you. They will see you as larger than life, and God will bless you by giving you influence. However, what people don't realize is behind the magnifying glass is a person who is small, just like a ladybug is tiny, but when viewed through a magnifying glass, it may look like a ferocious monster.

> *"Trying will never reach it, but there is an attitude where God puts you in faith in resting on His Word, a delighting inwardly over everything. I delight to do Thy will."* (Smith Wigglesworth, 1926)

God's blessing for the believer is not seen in the absence of resistance, but in the assurance of victory. David had a call on his life to destroy the enemies of Israel; as such his life pre-echoes that of the Messiah, who defeated sin, death, and the devil once and for all. Bless His holy name.

Jesus warned us of this when he said, ***"These things I have spoken to you, that in Me you may have peace. In the world you will have tribulation; but be of good cheer, I have overcome the world."*** (John 16:33) Our peace is not in the absence of opposition, but in the presence of Jesus. He is peace. This is important to digest and even embrace. It's a decision to say "God, I don't understand what's going on, but I'm going to stay in shalom no matter what comes at me." That's the faith attitude. It's not passively embracing suffering. It's the attitude that says "I am not going to lean on my own understanding, I'm going to stay in faith. Even if you throw me into the furnace, my God will can deliver me and I'll come out without even the smell of smoke on me."

Peter also echoed this reality, ***"Even gold is tested for genuineness by fire. The purpose of these trials is so that your trust's genuineness, which is far more valuable than perishable gold, will be judged worthy of praise, glory and honor at***

the revealing of Yeshua the Messiah." (1 Peter 1:7 CJB) All who live godly will face persecution. Don't let it discourage you. On the contrary, just determine to rejoice and run over the opposition like a Sherman tank. David faced tremendous opposition, but he stayed in faith and his breakthrough came at the right time. Your confidence is not misplaced because your trust is in the Most High God.

I was swimming recently on the beach in Herzliya, Israel. The waves were a bit bigger than usual and there were plenty of surfers out. I swam out, duck-diving under the waves to get to the impact zone. The impact zone is where the waves break and you get pounded if you stay there. You get tossed about, losing all control of your body, tumbling in the white water like the spin cycle in your washing machine. When you finally come up for a gasp of air, another wave comes crashing down over you. I think many believers are living their whole lives in the impact zone. What is needed is perseverance and faith to get past the impact zone to the line-up. We need to go through the impact zone before we can get to where we want to be. Keep moving in faith! Lord, deliver us in your grace from the impact zone. And let us not grow weary in doing good.

Returning to 2 Samuel 5, David went up against the Jebusites and took Jerusalem. From then on, it would be called the city of David. As he turns to face the Philistines in the Valley of Rephaim, the Valley of Giants, David got the victory over Israel's nemesis. The Valley of Giants would be called Baal Perazim, the Valley of Breakthrough.

Prerequisites for Breakthrough:

Step 1: Remember past victories. Coming to the Valley of Giants, David never forgot the day the Lord gave him victory over Goliath. When Adonai Tzva'ot shows up, it's never even a close fight.

Step 2: Be patient. David had numerous opportunities to blow it. He could have killed Saul on at least two occasions, but would not touch the Lord's anointed. Rather, he waited patiently for God to fulfil His promise. The fruit of the Spirit includes patience. When we are impatient, we are telling God through our actions that we are not satisfied with His provision. There is a place for holy dissatisfaction with the status quo, but David's heartfelt desire was first and foremost for the glory of God and the welfare of His people Israel.

Step 3: Inquire of the Lord. ***"So David inquired of the Lord, saying, 'Shall I go up against the Philistines? Will you deliver them into my hand?' And the Lord said to David, 'Go up, for I will doubtless deliver the Philistines into your hand.'"*** (2 Samuel 5:19)

Step 4: Do what God says. ***"So David went to Baal Perazim, and David defeated them there; and he said, 'The Lord has broken through my enemies before me, like a breakthrough of water.' Therefore he called the name of that place Baal Perazim."*** (2 Samuel 5:20)

The Fruit of Breakthrough:

Result 1: We know our Father more intimately as Jehovah Perazim, the Lord of Breakthrough. The victory of the cross becomes personal to us.

Result 2: We step into our divine destiny. The prophetic anointing of David was brought to fulfilment as he defeated the Philistines and consolidated all Israel and Judah under his rule.

Result 3: The enemies of the Lord are brought into disrepute. ***"And they left their images there, and David and his men carried them away."*** (2 Samuel 5:21)

Advantages We Have for Breakthrough:

Advantage 1: A new and better covenant, founded on better promises and ratified by the blood of Jesus.

Advantage 2: Jesus disarmed principalities and powers. ***"Having disarmed principalities and powers, He made a public spectacle of them, triumphing over them in it."*** (Colossians 2:15) The enemy of God's people can only resort to lies and accusations. He has no power over a believer unless, and until, we agree with his lies. However, we believe God's word and not the lies of the devil. We repudiate every accusation, even those we make against ourselves.

Advantage 3: We have the full counsel of the written Word of God; David had only a portion thereof in the Torah. We also have the Tanakh, the Gospels and the Epistles. We don't have to learn by the school of hard knocks if we are willing to submit and be instructed by the pure Word of God.

Advantage 4: David needed a breakthrough before he could be king, but we are kings already. The Torah strictly divided kingship and priesthood, but like Jesus, we are also priests. Through the victory of the cross, we are called to be priests and kings. ***"To Him who loved us and washed us from our sins in His own blood, and has made us kings and priests to His God and Father, to Him*** **be** ***glory and dominion forever and ever. Amen."*** (Revelation 1:5-6) Every born-again believer needs to know that the blood of Jesus makes us as holy as any Aaronic priest. His name makes us more powerful than any of David's mighty men.

KINGDOM PROCESS vs. LOTTO MENTALITY

Breakthrough may come in a moment, such as when David strengthened himself in the Lord in the narrative above, but this momentary breakthrough is usually connected with a process. This is why scripture promotes patience, endurance and perseverance. These qualities are under assault in our over-connected culture. Our instant gratification culture of consumerism stands in stark contrast to Kingdom principles. This generation has a lotto ticket mentality, that everything will be taken care of in an instant to deliver us from our poor choices. Nothing could be more ungodly or antithetical to the ways of the Kingdom. Patience, endurance, and perseverance are all derivatives of faith, and ***"Without faith, it is impossible to please Him for he who comes to God must believe that He is, and that He is a rewarder of those who diligently seek Him."*** (Hebrews 11:6)

To diligently seek Him is not something done as an afterthought for ten minutes in the morning while shaving and brushing our teeth. It means taking time where He is able to have our full attention and making Him a priority; ***"and your Father who sees in secret will Himself reward you openly."*** (Matthew 6:4) Can you imagine if we constantly told our wife and children we loved them, yet when they come begging to spend time with us, we let them know, "I can give you a few minutes while I get ready for the day. We can talk while I am getting dressed, brushing my teeth, and shaving. If you want more time than that, too bad."

When the Lord led Israel into the Promised Land, there was a process to be observed for their own good. Faith was demonstrated by trusting the Lord from moment to moment. Israel was constantly in a position that required them to depend on God. The fleshly nature doesn't like exposing itself to that kind of vulnerability, but clearly the Lord comes through much better than we ever could for ourselves. More than this, intimacy with the Lord is the fruit of such vulnerability.

> ***"And the Lord your God will drive out those nations before you little by little; you will be unable to destroy them at once, lest the beasts of the field become too numerous for you."***
> (Deuteronomy 7:22)

Here is the process: God speaks the Word, then by faith we cross the Jordan and receive our inheritance. By trust, we drive out our enemies one by one and possess the land. We receive salvation in a mere instant when we pray and open our heart and receive the Lord Jesus as Lord and Savior of our lives. While that breakthrough may happen in a matter of moments, it is connected with a greater process. Jesus was crucified before the foundation of the world. Before we ever had a need, God made the provision. In that moment of salvation, our old man dies and we are no longer slaves to sin and death. Isn't it wonderful? Jesus lived the life we should have lived. Jesus died the death we should have died, in our place. When we receive this "so great salvation," we are instantly changed in the Spirit. We are not only forgiven, we are credited with His righteousness. By agreeing with the Word of God by standing in faith, we draw out the things of the Spirit into our physical realm.

FROM INTERNSHIP TO TRANSFORMATION

As stated before, there are people in our workplace that only we can reach for the Lord. I was first introduced to Will through his brother, who asked me if I would consider hiring Will as a summer intern. At the time, Will was a student at a major university in Georgia and I was based in Zürich. I was going to spend Christmas in the Atlanta area with family, so I arranged to meet him. We met at a Starbucks in an Alpharetta strip-mall. After that meeting, I decided to step out in faith and fly Will to Zürich for the summer. Between our first interview and the start date, disaster struck in Will's life.

He made a terrible decision to get behind the wheel after drinking and was arrested for drunk driving. To make matters worse, this infraction led to him being expelled from one of the premier business schools in the US. We decided to bring him to Switzerland in spite of these things. When he arrived, he was despondent, seemingly lost, and had a terrible attitude. Underlying all of that was the pain of losing his father prematurely at the age of thirteen.

Will says of his experience: *"I felt alone, like a fatherless orphan. While I was still a long way off, God ran out to me, He embraced me and brought me into His family. What I thought was freedom had become bondage to me. What I had always thought of as bondage or 'religion' was actually my ultimate freedom; a relationship with Jesus Christ."*

After some weeks went by and we established a bit of a relationship, I asked Will if we could pray together. I dragged him along to a prayer meeting in Zürich. The Lord had moved in his heart. God wanted so much to pour out His love on Will, to heal and restore him, but he could not do it until Will was willing to receive it.

From that time, I've seen firsthand how God rocked Will's world. That young man got hungry for the Word and did a total 180 degree turn. Within a year of being arrested and kicked out of university, Will travelled to Switzerland, Indonesia, Australia, and New Zealand. He enrolled in another university and finished his degree in finance. He passed the National Commodities Futures Exam (Series 3) issued by the National Futures Association. He enrolled in YWAM Perth and went through Disciple Training School. There in Perth, Will met the girl of his dreams and they are now married.

Worldwide travel. Multiple degrees and professional designations. A beautiful, godly wife; does that sound like the résumé of a convicted drunk driver who was expelled from university? That's an awesome God-story.

Because of my business, I was uniquely positioned to play a small role in what God is doing in Will's life and he's one of my best friends to this day. I could plant some seeds, but God brought the growth.

When breakthrough comes, God's provision is always more than enough. That's just His abundant nature. Biblical examples abound. When God provided manna to Israel in the desert, they had more than they could eat. When the disciples multiplied the loaves and fish at the hands of Jesus, there was a huge overflow. When Jesus fed the 4,000, there were twelve large baskets left over. Likewise, with the feeding of the 5,000, there were five baskets collected after the miraculous provision. The prophet Elisha received provision from the widow in Zarephath while the rest of the land went without due to a famine. The only problem was she also had nothing. Yet, Jehovah Jireh is our provider; He met the needs of the widow and Elisha in an extravagant way.

Perhaps the heart of the Father is best displayed in the parable Jesus told of the prodigal son. When the younger brother repented and turned back to the father, we see the father lavished him. Not based on what he did, but based on who he was: his son. The father killed the fatted calf, threw a party, put his own robe on the son and a ring on his finger.

BREAKTHROUGH FOR A DIVORCED SINGLE MOM

Another amazing breakthrough I recently witnessed occurred in the life of Gloria, a Mexican lady who has a beautiful prophetic gift and walks with the Lord. However, after years of faithfulness, suddenly things seemingly started to unravel. Gloria found herself divorced and living in Switzerland, the country with the highest cost of living in the world, with no income and two children to support. She tried to get a job just about anywhere to make ends meet, but things just weren't coming through. To make things worse, her ex-husband lost his job and was unable to make any alimony payments. When these things happen, we can get bitter or better, as they say.

Gloria attended our weekly prayer meeting in Zürich, after a seemingly random connection to me on LinkedIn. I didn't need the gift of discernment to know how deeply in anguish she was. We made an appointment to meet at my office for prayer. As always, I keep my door open or simply meet in a public place to avoid any appearance of impropriety. In general, if a lady needs ministry, I refer her to another lady, but in this case, I felt led by the Spirit to minister to Gloria.

As we prayed, Gloria was led to completely forgive her ex-husband. I had a profound sense of how the Lord was also deeply in anguish for her and His heart overflowed with compassion. Over the following months we prayed together, but the situation seemed to get worse. Her situation felt so desperate I couldn't imagine how God would intervene. There were months when Gloria's bank account was completely empty, and we just had to believe God for rent and groceries. To add pressure to the situation, her residence permit had expired. She needed to find a job or face imminent deportation. All through this struggle, the real miracle was how much Gloria blessed the people around her, especially me.

Here is a picture of trust: with about 160 francs left in her bank account one month, Gloria brought her two children to the computer and showed them the balance. She said, "Kids, we are going to take the last amount we have and honor the Lord with it."

She felt led to give the last of her money in the offering at church. And you know what? The Lord came through for Gloria in ways that were beyond what we could ask or think. Within a year of that first prayer meeting in my office, Gloria was engaged to be married to a successful businessman and pastor. ***"Weeping may endure for a night, but joy comes in the morning."*** (Psalm 30:5) She has since relocated to the US, her children are enrolled in excellent private Christian schools and life has dramatically changed for her. She continues to be a blessing to me as we pray together on the phone regularly.

FROM ILLITERATE BRICKLAYER TO BILLIONAIRE

The testimony of Peter Daniels of Adelaide, South Australia is astounding. At the age of twenty-six, he was working as a bricklayer in Australia when he attended a Billy Graham crusade. Peter accepted Jesus Christ as his Lord and Savior that day in 1959. Prior to this, he had been practically illiterate, suffering from dyslexia.

Without education, without literacy, coming from a broken home, having several relatives in jail or on welfare for generations, the prognosis for Peter's career was not altogether optimistic. Yet, when he accepted Jesus as Lord and Savior, something rose up on the inside of him: a realization that he was the equal of all men before God.

Peter went on a lifelong journey to "see how much money one could give away in one's life." First, he put a dictionary by his bed and in the bathroom. He carried a third dictionary around, asking people to explain what the words meant. Eventually, he learned every word in the dictionary. He also read 2,000 biographies during those early years. Peter started a business. The first business failed, the second failed, and so did the third. His wife pleaded with him to give up and just get a normal job. Still, he persevered, and the fourth business became massively successful with offices in Australia, Singapore, and Hong Kong. I believe God is raising up countless numbers of people like this who are called to be salt and light in the marketplace. Peter went on to build several successful businesses, serve on the boards of several international ministries, author thirteen books and be named by Norman Vincent Peale as the best public speaker in the world. He credits his success to Jesus Christ.

GOD BREAKS THE TOUGHEST ADDICTIONS

I was raised in a Christian home and attended church and Sunday school throughout my formative years. Nonetheless, I spent a large portion of my teenage years and young adult life living like the prodigal son. God restored me in a number of wonderful and life changing ways. His mercy endures forever. As mentioned earlier in the book, I was spared in several major terrorist incidents. On September 11, 2001, I missed work at my office on the 73rd floor of the World Trade Center because I got food poisoning from eating bad sushi the day before. In November 2008, I missed the terror attack at the Taj hotel in Mumbai simply because of a slipped disc that morning. God knew how to get my attention! He has a plan for my life and, therefore, protected me miraculously, even when I was not walking by the Spirit. He leads me in paths of righteousness for His names' sake.

I can also testify that I had suffered with a severe alcohol problem in those years. Let my shame be for His glory. It began in my high school years and got stronger and more difficult to control over time. You may wonder how I maintained a successful career on Wall St. while simultaneously struggling with a drinking problem. The fact is, the two seem to go together very well, up to a point. Entertaining partners and clients is part of the job description. By my mid-twenties, I had a massive income, travelled all over the world, enjoyed really the best of everything … but I was overweight, stressed out and hung over most of the time. I tried to stop in my own strength and couldn't do it. The alcohol curse is prevalent in my extended family and across generations.

Around that time, I became aware that George W. Bush (#43) had also suffered from a severe drinking problem. Nowhere near to the extent that I had probably, but nonetheless alcohol abuse was a legitimate threat to his future. Even with his family connections, Bush would never have made it to the presidency if he had kept drinking. Bush himself acknowledged in a recent interview: "I realized that alcohol was beginning to crowd out my energies and could crowd, eventually, my affections for other people . . . When you're drinking, it can be an incredibly selfish act." I had the opportunity to meet President Bush while he was still in office at the annual NRCC dinner in Washington D.C. Bush exuded a strong charisma along with a firm handshake. He was able to step into his destiny because he quit drinking. He decided his family and his future were more important. Bush's decision to quit drinking coincided with what he describes as a reawakening of his faith. God's grace is able to destroy even the worst addiction. Looking at Bush's example made it clear to me that I could choose alcohol and lose everything I hold dear, or I could choose life and blessing.

In those days, I lived in Singapore just a stone's throw from Sri Temasek, the Prime Minister's official residence. One Sunday, I woke up massively hung over, staggering from church to church, randomly walking in, sitting down in a pew, closing my eyes for a bit and walking on. I went into several empty churches that morning. Finally, I walked into one just as the service was starting. Impeccable timing, so I stayed. Afterwards, the young pastor said that if anyone needed prayer, please come up to the altar after the service. Boy, I sure needed prayer. So I went up there and I told that young Singaporean pastor everything. I told him that I had been drinking, that it was self-destructive, and that I was unable to stop. I was ashamed and scared. I can't remember exactly what he prayed as I was sobbing. The pastor laid his hands on me in the name of Jesus. As he did so, it was as if warm oil was poured all over me. It was incredibly comforting. Only in retrospect can I look back and realize that was the Holy Spirit. Abba broke the power of the curse. I was completely and supernaturally delivered from alcoholism. After that I never had to struggle at all, never had to attend any meetings. I am just totally set free. I am not merely an alcoholic in recovery; I am a totally brand new creature in Christ Jesus! Nothing is impossible for our God.

Prayer: *Spirit of truth, you know the area in my life where I need a breakthrough. I trust you to bring it to pass in your own perfect time. Help me to be patient and to persevere until then. I open my heart to you and give you permission to deal with anything in there that is standing between me and the destiny you have for me. In the beautiful name of Jesus, Amen.*

Meditation VIII

Wealth: Principles for Abundance

"'The silver is Mine, and the gold is Mine,' says the Lord of hosts." (Haggai 2:8)

"Investing is simple but not easy." (Warren Buffett)

Just as God makes the sun shine on both the wicked and the righteous, so too does He provide general principles for the protection and growth of wealth. These include diversification and compound interest. Anyone can take advantage of these basic financial principals.

Financial principles, like most natural laws, function regardless of one's character or belief system. Even if you don't believe in gravity, 9.8m/s squared is holding you down regardless of what you think of it. Most financial principles are like that. If one saves $1,000 per year for forty years with a six percent rate of return, the future value will be $154,761.97. That's an investment of just $83.33 per month, like the price of an extra cell phone bill. It's simply a matter of diligently saving a finite amount of money constantly and persistently. The exciting part is that virtually everybody can save a small amount of money consistently over a long period of time.

The not-so-thrilling part of financial laws are that they are equally destructive in reverse. Compounding high rates of debt will guarantee poverty; credit card debt and check cashing services are practical examples of how this works. Small amounts of money at negative rates of interest consistently, over a long period of time equals someone else becoming rich. The financial rules are no more moral or immoral than the law of gravity. It's simply a matter of how they are applied.

Below is a non-exhaustive list of financial principals that you can start applying practically today:

- Law of compounding returns. Compound interest is what Albert Einstein referred to as the most powerful force in the universe. Dynastic wealth is built primarily through compound interest. The main ingredients needed are a long time period and patience. Be highly skeptical on any investment opportunity that promises significant returns in a short period and require the investor to act quickly. ***"A good man leaves an inheritance to his children's children, but the wealth of the sinner is stored up for the righteous."*** (Proverbs 13:22) Think long-term and use the law of compound returns to build a multi-generational legacy.

- Limit losses. Traders often use a stop order to ensure that losses are limited. The reason this is so important is because if you lose ten percent, you need to make eleven percent to break even. However, the bigger the loss, the greater the risk required to break even. A negative twenty percent loss takes twenty-five percent to break even, negative thirty percent takes forty-two percent to break even, and negative forty percent requires sixty-six percent to break even. This explains why even though the stock market had strong returns from 2009 through 2017; most investors had to wait more than five years just to break even on losses sustained in 2008, when the Dow Jones, S&P 500, and Dax had losses of -33.83%, -38.49%, -40.37%, respectively.

  I should point out that limiting losses is exactly contrary to human psychology. Most people do not want to realize a loss; they will "hold and hope" or double down. On the contrary, as soon as they make a small profit, they are inclined to "lock it in." This pattern ensures that over time, average losses will be far greater in magnitude than the average winning trades.

- Avoid debt. Pay off credit cards in full each month. Pass on business ideas that absolutely depend on credit. This is the heritage of God's people: ***"You shall lend to many nations, but you shall not borrow."*** (Deuteronomy 28:12) It's not necessarily wrong to borrow money, but think of what it means: borrowing shows the Lord that you are not content with His current level of provision.

  As a testimony, I can share I've never had a loan or any debt, personally or in business. ***"Owe no one anything except to love one another."*** (Romans 13:8) If you absolutely need to borrow, any loan entered into must be fixed, not floating. That is to say, the amount you owe should not suddenly increase when interest rates go up. Avoid adjustable rate mortgages for example, even if they seem cheaper in the short run.

- Cash is king. Have a significant amount of cash reserves at all times. This means cash which is not pledged as collateral and is liquid. Cash reserves are important for unforeseen emergencies, but also for taking advantage of interesting investment opportunities as they arise.

- Hard assets. Personally, I keep a large amount of gold and silver, both physical and in the form of securities, such as ETFs. Precious metals are likely to maintain purchasing power over the next century in a way that no paper currencies can do over the long run. If you look over the past century, the largest, most liquid currencies were the US Dollar, British Pound, German Reichsmark and Japanese Yen. Needless to say, the Reichsmark became worthless through hyperinflation and was eventually replaced by the Deutschmark, which later was replaced by the Euro. Though the USD, GBP, and JPY have survived nominally, each of these lost most of their purchasing power over the past century, making cash an extremely poor generational store of value. An ounce of gold, on the other hand, could be traded for a stable amount of goods and services throughout not only the past century, but over thousands of years. This purchasing power is well protected in times of crisis. In 2008, I purchased huge amounts of gold and silver. I bought silver at ten dollars per ounce and sold less than two years later for forty dollars per ounce, making a 300% return.

- Generosity. Many will say, "I just can't afford to give right now." No, you can't afford *not* to give! Although it has been abused, there is a law of sowing and reaping. ***"Give, and it will be given to you: good measure, pressed down, shaken together, and running over will be put into your bosom. For with the same measure that you use, it will be measured back to you."*** (Luke 6:38) It's a biblical principal. The way of the world is to allocate income first to needs, then to wants, then to saving and investing and perhaps to giving if any is left over. The biblical way is to give first, as the number one priority. The first fruits are for the Lord. After that, automatically save and invest right off the top. The remainder is for fixed living expenses and, lastly, for variable expenses. Honor the Lord first. It's a matter of priority. ***"Honor the Lord with your possessions, and with the firstfruits of all your increase; so your barns will be filled with plenty, and your vats will overflow with new wine."*** (Proverbs 3:9-10)

- Budgeting. Most people never become wealthy regardless of their income level. This is because as soon as their income level increases, variable spending rises as well. They never save enough or have enough left over to give. The priority is always to consume, to buy a better car, bigger house, and other stuff. By faith, work out a budget for your household that prioritizes giving and saving. Ask the Lord for the discipline to limit variable spending.

- Recognize and eliminate emotional bias when investing or making any purchasing decision. Market trends are almost always based on fear and greed. Bull markets are a manifestation of greed when securities prices become unhinged from any underlying economic reality. Conversely, bear markets are the result of collective fear when prices become artificially cheap compared to real economic value. One of my traders says, "If you are going to panic, make sure to panic early or not at all."

- Diversify. There has never been a time in history when private investors had access to such a vast array of investment opportunities and asset classes with such deep liquidity and low transaction costs. We recommend investors not only have a diversified asset allocation, but also have a varied entry point. Consider dollar cost averaging. For example, if one wishes to purchase 100,000 shares of XYZ stock, consider regularly purchasing 10,000 shares every month or quarter until the desired amount is accumulated. This takes the guesswork out of the entry point and ensures that when the price of the stock goes down, one is acquiring a greater number of units.

- Low correlation. Good portfolio construction will always look at the correlation of the investments, preferring to add securities when they have a low correlation to other portfolio constituents, hence further reducing the expected volatility and maximum loss. Notice we are looking for investments with low correlation, not negative correlation. Negative correlation means that the investments vary inversely. For example, the older men get, the less hair they tend to have; men's age and hair are negatively correlated. What is more interesting is to have investments with a low correlation, which means that there is no statistical relationship in their price history. Most equities have a positive correlation, meaning that they rise and fall together.

- Derivatives. FX, futures, and options markets are typically highly leveraged. Unless you are a bona fide hedger or a professional trader, you probably don't want to get involved in trading derivatives. This is an excellent example of the Pareto principle: twenty percent of the professional traders make eighty percent of the trading profits, whereas eighty percent of retail investors lose money. My experience is this: don't trade FX ever; only the banks win. Don't trade options ever, except for perhaps a conservative covered call strategy. Strategies trading futures can be interesting because they often have low correlation to stocks and bonds. Futures trading strategies are best accessed through regulated investment managers who offer transparent investment funds or separately managed accounts to access these markets.

HANDLING WEALTH ON THE FAR SIDE OF THE CROSS

> ***"But the wealth of the sinner is stored up for the righteous."*** (Proverbs 13:22)

Above we looked at some general financial principles, which can be put to use by anyone and they will work over time. Simple, but not easy. We must admit, however, there is more to consider here than just money. The Scripture expressly says, ***"For the love of money is a root of all kinds of evil."*** (1 Timothy 6:10)

My assertion is that without the redemptive work of Jesus Christ, the allure of money will ultimately enslave and destroy you. If you think money won't affect you, you've probably never handled a large amount of it. I can tell you first hand that large amounts of money will tend to exaggerate one's character flaws. I made a tremendous income by my mid-twenties working on Wall Street. By age twenty-six, I was a managing director in a multi-billion dollar hedge fund with a corner office overlooking Park Avenue. I'm not proud of some of the mistakes I made in those days. Praise the Lord for His faithfulness and grace in restoring me.

We all know rich people who are extremely unhappy, loaded down with worries such as their children at each other's throats over the inheritance, etc. I know a wealth manager in Tel Aviv who keeps a psychologist on staff to help his wealthy clients cope with all their neurological disorders. He says the most important thing to keep in the conference room is plenty of boxes of tissues. The spirit of Mammon offers empty consumerism, meaningless materialism and an insatiable appetite for more stuff. This is why our Lord Jesus made it emphatically clear in the Sermon on the Mount: ***"No one can serve two masters; for either he will hate the one and love the other, or else he will be loyal to the one and despise the other. You cannot serve God and mammon"*** (Matthew 6:24). How are you making your major life decisions? Are they based on what God says or what money dictates?

This is important stuff. Money is an important factor in our daily life, no way around it. I believe the Lord's heart is for us to be empowered to handle and disburse massive wealth and other resources for the great ingathering. I absolutely believe God wants me to prosper in everything I set my hand to, but only when He, the Lord of my life, is securely in place on the throne of my heart, can I be truly trusted to handle wealth. Why? If God's not on the throne of your heart, Mammon and other idols, like success and power, will move right in and set up shop. Anything wrong with success and power? No. Can they be perverted and abused and misused? Absolutely. Same thing for money. With Christ alone reigning in my heart, money becomes what it truly is: just a means of exchange that will pass away. It is temporal and valuable, it can be traded or invested for other temporal things or even eternal things. It's one thing to say you believe in something you cannot immediately prove. It's another level of faith altogether when you invest dollars for the sake of the Kingdom and eternity. That's the real deal. Faith without works is dead; a look through one's financial statements will show what they love and believe in.

Wealth and resources can be generated supernaturally, and there are biblical examples of this. For instance, Israel received gifts from the Egyptians on their way out of the country. That silver and gold jewelry was later used to finance the building of the ark. Apparently, the runaway slave nation was so wealthy in the desert that Moses had to command them to stop giving! In 2004, Joan Kroc of the McDonald's fortune gave a $1.5 billion gift to the Salvation Army. How wonderful!

If you're like me, you've prayed Proverbs 13:22 many times: ***"the wealth of the sinner is stored up for the righteous."*** There's nothing wrong with that prayer, and yet I believe God has a better way that requires us to walk by faith, depending on Him for each step.

While a supernatural wealth transfer has biblical precedent, the more common path to wealth creation is a product of God's blessing, hard work, and time. ***"And you shall remember the Lord your God, for it is He who gives you the power to get wealth***" (Deuteronomy 8:18). The best way to create wealth is to discover the gifts God has given you, develop them, and use them to serve and bless others. People are willing to compensate for good service, high quality, innovation and excellent value.

Honor God first. Where your heart is, there will your treasure be. It's another way of saying: one's spending habits are a direct reflection of the desires of your heart. Honor God with your first fruits, then allocate to savings. Many people build elaborate investment plans, but fail to understand that saving regularly is a much more important factor in wealth accumulation than simply picking the right investment strategy.

VELOCITY OF MONEY

God hates stagnation. Flow! One important, and yet rarely discussed, economic indicator is the velocity of money. This represents the frequency at which the same unit of currency is used to purchase new goods and services within a given period of time. The health of an economy is vastly determined by the velocity of monetary turnover. Economic downturns start when investors and consumers starting hoarding wealth. I like the thought of the money in my pocket flowing through the hands of those in my community, blessing small and great alike. I think God likes that too.

The parable of the rich fool is told by Jesus and recorded in Luke's 12: ***"The ground of a certain rich man yielded an abundant harvest. He thought to himself, 'what shall I do? I have no place to store my crops.'"*** Notice that it was the ground that produced the abundance, not the man himself.

And he continues, ***"This is what I'll do. I will tear down my barns and build bigger ones, and there I will store my***

surplus grain. And I'll say to myself, 'You have plenty of grain laid up for many years. Take life easy; eat, drink and be merry.'" Notice where the rich fool puts his trust: in stored up wealth. How does he allocate this wealth? Merely by his own carnal appetite.

What's God's view of this self-centered wealth stagnation? ***"But God said to him 'you fool! This very night your life will be demanded from you. Then who will get what you prepared for yourself?' This is how it will be with whoever stores up things for themselves and is not rich toward God."*** Hardcore, right?

God is not playing games. Is God in a bad mood? What's the problem here? The grain silo sounds like an ancient version of a retirement account or pension fund. Is there a problem with saving for retirement and saving for the future? Of course not. This is a matter of the heart. The rich fool fails to acknowledge the source of his abundance. He fails to consider anyone but himself. One need not look further than the patriarchs to know God isn't bothered about His children having nice stuff. He is interested in the heart. The rich fool should have acknowledged God with the first fruits. It's a matter of priority. It's a matter of using wealth to bless in a tangible way those whom you claim to love as yourself.

We know God is not opposed merely to the accumulation of grain or wealth because Joseph, at God's leading, did just that. The Scripture records perhaps the greatest supernatural wealth transfer in history when Joseph went from the prison to the palace. From literally having nothing in prison to managing all the wealth and power of the world's greatest superpower of the time, Egypt. As the de facto prime minister, I'm sure Joseph had a fine home, wore good clothes appropriate to his position and dined sumptuously. However, Joseph always acknowledged God first and when his time finally came, he used his power and wealth wisely to bless a starving nation and to fulfill divine purpose in bringing Israel down to Egypt.

How often have I been the rich fool, presumptuous, wasteful, inconsiderate, not stopping for a millisecond to consider the source or give thanks? Thank you, Lord Jesus. Rich beyond measure, He spent all He had for a wretch like me. How can I boast? What do I have that I haven't been given?

THE GREATEST INVESTOR

The parable of the talents shows God is an investor. While God's love and grace is offered freely to all, this is not to say He looks on everyone the same. When it comes to dispensing His blessings, God is looking for a good return on His investment. What does this mean? Never forget God is first and foremost interested in the eternal, especially the destiny of people.

Sadly, there are many people whom God wants to bless, including financially, but does not do so because He sees they are not a good investment. What God will do is give a person a little bit of money to see how they handle it. He's looking for a faithful steward who does not squander it and keeps track of where it goes, then He knows He can entrust this person with greater riches. The biblical principle is: ***"He who is faithful in what is least is faithful also in much; and he who is unjust in what is least is unjust in also in much."*** (Luke 16:10)

When you get your paycheck, can you account for where every penny out of it goes? I realize you may be aware of the major items like a mortgage or rental payment and insurance, but what about the small items? If God cannot trust you with the small things, He will not trust you with big things.

A young airman in the Air Force came to understand this concept loud and clear. He served as a tail gunner on a B-52 during the height of the Cold War. He recalled his time in training: before being assigned to an actual aircraft, how every day, a senior NCO would come to their room for inspection.

The Air Force, like all branches of the military, have a regulation for everything. They have a regulation for how to fold your socks, shirts, underwear, how much space should be between each shirt hanging up, the direction they are to face, how much space between socks, and so on.

The inspector would inevitably fail them for some minor infraction such as a pair of folded socks being one-eighth of an inch too wide. Of course, it was always frustrating, especially after spending a large amount of time preparing, only to fail for something seemingly so trivial. Finally, one time after failing because a pair of his underwear was not perfectly square, he couldn't take it anymore. He raised his voice to the instructor and said, "We are here to work on a B-52 that carries nuclear weapons. What difference does it make how our underwear is folded? This is stupid."

The instructor's answer changed his life.

"Son, you want us to trust you to be responsible for a multi-million dollar aircraft, entrust you with the most powerful weapons the world has ever seen—weapons that can destroy the world. You want us to do this when we can't even trust you to fold your own underwear?"

> ***"He who did not spare His own Son, but delivered Him up for us all, how shall he not with Him also freely give us all things?"*** (Romans 8:32)

By His poverty, we are rich. You can spiritualize this if you want, but I'm going to thank God for the abundance and wealth He has given me and my family to enjoy. I have enough for all the needs of my house and an overflow for every good work. If you have a heart to impact the world for Jesus, He will flow many resources through you. TD Jakes says, "If He can get it through you, He'll get it to you." We are blessed to be a blessing and it's time for the church to be emancipated from the poverty mentality. According to 2 Corinthians 8:9, ***"For you know the grace of our Lord Jesus Christ, that, though he was rich, yet for your sakes he became poor, that you through his poverty might be rich."***

Bread for the eater and seed for the sower; God gives us enough for both and the proportion between what you consume (bread for the eater) and what you invest (seed for sowing) is between you and Him. I can only say it would be pretty stupid to eat all your seed. Put your capital to work for this life and the age to come. Don't work for money; make money work for you!

MAKING AN IMPACT

You won't see it in the news, but the church is having massive impact on the world. I was in Mumbai and my Hindu friend said, "Thank God for the Christians or there would be no one to take care of our poor!" While I appreciate his compliment, I could not help but think that this impact we were having was limited by our poverty mentality, thinking our funds were limited, instead of realizing when we receive things, we are drawing on His immutable faithfulness and abundant grace. Instead of relying on ourselves or the good works of others, imagine if we begin to partner our faith with what God is doing!

The Bible declares God owns the cattle on a thousand hills. An asteroid in our solar system was recently discovered and is composed almost entirely of nickel and iron that has an estimated market value of $10 quintillion. That's a 1 followed by nineteen zeroes. By comparison, a trillion only has twelve zeroes. As a son or daughter of God, we are royalty, a prince or princess, and heir to all that wealth plus so much more. We do not need to live with a mentality of wondering how we are going to get by. When our backs are to the Red Sea and our worst fear has hedged us in regarding finances, He makes a way!

In John 2, Jesus showed us what He envisioned the relationship between earthly wealth and His kingdom to be. Being the creator of all things (John 1:2), He made business for the church, not the church for business. Jesus made a whip of cords and drove out the money changers. What is important to note is He was not angry because of the services they were offering;

His problem was they were profaning a sacred place for gain and charging an exorbitant fee for their services.

There is nothing wrong with having something of value to offer to others; it is a practical necessity for all of us, since we don't have the time to manufacture all the things we need on our own. The congregation is not to be viewed merely as a pool of prospects we can use to enrich ourselves. We are called to feed the sheep, not fleece the sheep. We can discern the spirit of deception in the local body of believers when we see a person profit excessively from the house of God. There is nothing wrong with profit in a general sense. If an item is sold "at cost," there is no incentive to engage in research and go the extra mile. The Bible says, ***"the laborer is worthy of his hire,"*** (Luke 10:7) so receiving compensation for your work is Scriptural, but the problem is some people take advantage of this.

Let us not be distracted by or even jealous of the many "rich fools" around us. It's tempting to look at the wicked of the world, who appear to be prospering, but we are expressly told not to be envious of those who do wrong. Why not? ***"For like the grass they will soon whither, like green plants they will soon die away … For evil men will be cut off, but those who hope in the Lord will inherit the land."*** (Psalm 37:2,9 NIV)

Proverbs 10:22 says, ***"The blessing of the Lord makes one rich, and He adds now sorrow with it."*** There is a blessing from which includes, but is not limited to, material blessing. The enemy is described as the god of this age, who has blinded the minds of the unbelieving. He also has a certain capacity to allocate money, power, and other things of the world. Why? He received that authority when he usurped Adam's delegated role of dominion. That is why the Christ had to come as the Son of Man; only as a human could He reclaim what mankind had woefully given up. So, we live in a contradictory age where two powerful forces are present and clashing. Suffice it to say that when the enemy bestows money, it is for his own deceitful purposes. It's never to build up, but to destroy.

The Lord is calling out men and women of valor, to whom He can entrust true wealth. Maybe He is speaking to your heart right now. Will you respond to the call and rise to the occasion? Those who would use wealth not merely for personal benefit but would instead use it to advance His Kingdom first. God has nothing against business—in fact, the Bible has much to say about this subject. His concern is, will you let money rule you, or will you rule over your money? It is not money that is the root of all evil, but the ***"love of money is the root of all evil."*** (1 Timothy 6:10)

DISTRIBUTION OF WEALTH

One thing we must remember is that unlike today's social justice concepts of wealth distribution and equal outcomes, God's provision is perfect and righteous, though completely different from a human view of equality.

While a common phrase is that all men were created equal, we must be careful what we mean by that. When the phrase is used in America's Declaration of Independence, the founding fathers knew that was not literally true. Some people are born blind, deaf, or without fingers, a hand, or leg. Some are born into wealth with two loving parents, while others are born into poverty with parents more interested in their own lusts than raising a child.

When the Bible says God is no respecter of persons, it does not mean all men are equal in circumstances. Instead, it is referring to all of us having the same equal opportunity to walk with God and in His blessings. Regardless of where you came from, you can access the wealth God has to offer to you as His child. There are too many stories to count of people who grew up in poverty or seemingly hopeless situations, only to go on to achieve greatness.

God distributes His wealth based on not just need, but on how wise you will be with it. We see a good example of this in Numbers 7. In the chapter, the princes of Israel brought an offering of six covered wagons and twelve oxen. The offering was to be distributed to those from the tribe of Levi, who were the priestly class. While they received certain benefits like the offering, they were not given portions of land like the other tribes were.

Among the Levites were three families: the Gershon, Merari, and Kothan. What is interesting is that the offering was not split up equally between them. Gershon was given two carts and four oxen. Merari was given four carts and eight oxen, while Kothan did not receive anything. We are not sure exactly why the goods were distributed in this way, but it probably had to do with the duties each of them were assigned to do. What is worth noting is that there is never any record of any members of the tribe of Levi lacking food or any other provision. The lesson here is that God will provide for whatever He calls you to do.

We see other examples of this principle found in the Bible. While in the wilderness, Moses struck the rock the first time and it brought forth water to meet the needs of all the Jewish people in the desert. Paul said this rock followed them wherever they went and that it was Jesus Christ (1 Corinthians 10:4). Striking the rock was a picture of Jesus being ***"bruised for our transgressions."*** (Isaiah 53:5) When they needed water again, Moses was told this time to just speak to the rock to get the water. This is because Jesus was only offered once for our sins, never to die again. Also, by speaking, it shows God's intention is for us to receive our provision not by our strength, but by the spoken word of faith. In John 2, we see another picture of God's abundance by the miraculous provision of new and better wine.

When God blesses, it's always more than enough. When the people of Israel complained about the manna they were given, He sent them quail in the desert that was so abundant, it was up to their waists. Twice Jesus fed the multitudes; five-thousand one time with five loaves and four-thousand another time with seven loaves. Afterward, there were twelve and seven baskets left over, respectively. God's blessing can't be refined to a formula and it is much than enough for every need.

During a time of famine, a widow was in danger of losing everything to pay for the debts left by her husband. The creditors were even going to take her son as a slave. The man of God, Elisha, told her to get every container and pot she could get ahold of. Then she was told to take the small containers she had and fill them all up with oil. The small jug filled all the containers up to the brim. She was then told to sell the oil and pay off her debts. The miracle administered by Elisha not only got her out of debt, but there was more than enough provision for her livelihood.

I should point out that many of the objects of popular secular idolatry are not bad things. As stated before, money is a great servant but a terrible master. There is nothing wrong with success, money, or sex under the covenant of marriage. These are wonderful blessings from our Father! However, when we elevate these things to a place of importance reserved only for Christ, bad things happen.

The good news is you don't have to quit your investment banking job. It must, however, be subordinated to the order God intended. Your job should have no more and no less importance than its rightful place. It is more important than your car and less important than your family.

Examining our lives looking for idols is hard work because we are innately blind to them. That's our nature; it's built into how we operate. The Bible calls this our "flesh." Isaiah says those who seek the Lord will not do so in vain. Let's cast out our idols and proclaim Jesus Lord of our lives! If it is true that one day every knee will bow before the Lord, perhaps we should start in earnest now.

To whom do you kneel? It's commonly believed Christianity is the largest religion in the world while Islam is the fastest growing. This is at best a surface level observation. I submit that most people are polytheists, alternately worshipping wealth, power, and sex. Self-deification fanned by pride is popular.

If you doubt this, how does one explain working sixty hours a week in glass and metal skyscrapers, sacrificing personal health and family time on the altar of success? Isn't the modern trinity the CEO, board, and majority shareholder? Would it ever occur to us that reaching for the iPhone to return emails on a Saturday afternoon is a twisted kind of worship?

Prayer: *Lord God, thank you for your love. I confess that in the area of finances and prosperity, I have often relied on my own strength and succumbed to anxiety and fear. Lord, I want to do finances your way from now on. I acknowledge you as the source of every good thing in my life. In Jesus' name. Amen.*

Meditation IX

Purity: Taking the Trash Out

> ***"Draw near to God and He will draw near to you. Cleanse your hands, you sinners; and purify your hearts, you double-minded."*** (James 4:8)

One night, I dreamed that my family and I were in a beautiful, rugged mountain range. As I looked down into the valley I saw a wide and beautiful winding river. Upon a closer look, I was shocked to see that the river was completely stagnant, not flowing at all, as if it was frozen in time. I hiked down to its banks, knelt down, and prayed. As I prayed the river started moving, slowly at first, then the current began to accelerate until it became rushing rapids. My little girls were up above, laughing and cheering me on.

> ***"He who believes in Me, as the Scripture has said, out of his heart will flow rivers of living water."*** (John 7:38)

Even when nothing appears to be moving around you, rest assured, your faith soaked prayers are moving things in heaven, where the river of God proceeds from His throne. ***"And he showed me a pure river of water of life, clear as crystal, proceeding from the throne of God and of the Lamb."*** (Revelation 22:1)

Then I heard a voice: "You have enough fire. You don't need to ask for any more. Instead of more fire, use the fire that you have been given." Spiritual download: I then realized the truth that a tiny little flame can light hundreds of candles all around us. Also, a single candle can be seen from nearly a mile-and-a-half away on a clear night. The beauty of the Kingdom is the infinity of our resource. I am able to light hundreds of candles, yet my own light source is not diminished, it only grows brighter. This is because the Kingdom operates by infinite love. Worldly resources are limited, but Kingdom resources are unlimited when the love of the Father is manifested.

When I started my business, I invested what was a relatively small sum of money (but it was a large amount to me). Years later, that small investment has grown to where it now blesses so many accountants, lawyers, banks, brokers, auditors, regulators, tax authorities, graphic designers, distributors, and other service providers, all of whom make fee income from my business. Rather than diminishing, my investment has grown many times over to where it now provides revenue for other businesses, enabling them to make payroll.

This multiplication principle is repeated throughout Scripture; you can't miss it. When Elisha came to the widow who had no money to pay off her debts, he asked her to use what little oil she had left. As she honored the prophet's command, the Lord began filling bowl after bowl after bowl until she had more than enough. *God multiplies what we already have!*

In the same way, Jesus blessed and distributed the five loaves and two fishes. He used the small amount they had on hand. The abundance was so great that twelve baskets of leftovers were picked up. Hallelujah. *God multiplies what we already have!*

Likewise, in the parable of the talents, those who multiplied their talents stepped out in faith, trading what they had. *God multiplies what we already have!*

> ***"Then the Lord said to him, 'What is that in your hand?'"***
>
> ***"'A staff,' he replied."*** (Exodus 4:2)

Let's use what we've got!

For to him who has, more will be given. Take inventory, what have you got in your temple? Faith, hope and love. Ask God to multiply them today!

> ***"Peace to you!" Then He said to Thomas, "Reach your finger here, and look at My hands; and reach your hand here, and put it into My side. Do not be unbelieving, but believing." And Thomas answered and said to Him, "My Lord and my God!"*** (John 20:27-28)

Like Thomas, we too proclaim, "My Lord and my God." Even though we have not seen, we have felt him . . . we have felt the presence of the Lord. All doubt and unbelief melt away as we continuously proclaim, "My Lord and my God."

> ***Jesus said to him, "Thomas, because you have seen Me, you have believed. Blessed are those who have not seen and yet have believed."*** (John 20:29)

Hear the longing in the Father's voice as He calls us to ever higher heights. His love is calling us beyond what we could previously see or comprehend. Upon opening the eyes of our heart, we gaze upon the pure, the honorable, and the lovely. Seated with Him in heavenly places, executors of His will on earth.

We are not limited to the sum of our talents, abilities, circumstances, and resources. The Lord of Heaven says, ***"Blessed are those who have not seen and yet have believed."*** (John 20:29) The Father provides everything we need to fulfill our calling and divine destiny.

His grace enables us to walk in a spirit of excellence. What does it look like when the *talmidim* in the marketplace seek Him with all their heart? (Talmidim תלמידים–A plural Hebrew noun meaning "disciples" in its truest sense: those who leave family to study and follow the ways of their teacher [rabbi]. They study not only to learn what their teacher knows but to become the type of man their teacher is. Singular: talmid. Source: Psalm 119 Foundation)

Manifesting the Father's heart through an excellent spirit:

- Imagine today all the sick and brokenhearted congregating at the marketplace to receive a divine touch. ***"They laid the sick in marketplaces, and begged Him that they might just touch the hem of His garment. And as many as touched Him were made well."*** (Mark 6:56)

- Visualize the excellence of Solomon's kingdom, which drew royalty to him like a magnet. The Queen of Sheba being the most notable, having seen ***"all the wisdom of Solomon, the house that he has built, the food on his table, the seating of his servants, the service of his waiters and their apparel, his cupbearers, and his entryway by which he went up to the house of the Lord, there was no more spirit it her."*** (1 Kings 10:4) Yes, imagine it. Working heartily unto the Lord with such excellence, intricacy, and attention to detail that God is honored. A level of excellence that takes the CEO's breath away, which makes our clients say, ***"indeed the half was not told me. Your wisdom and prosperity exceed the fame of which I heard."*** (1 Kings 10:8)

- What if we, like Daniel, had such a relationship with God, such an anointing in the Spirit, that it was said of us: ***"In every matter of wisdom and understanding about which the king questioned them, he found them ten times better than all the magicians and enchanters in his whole kingdom?"*** (Daniel 1:20)

I'll take for granted that we all want to manifest one-hundred percent excellence in our work. Sign me up, right? Where do we start, practically speaking?

Let's look at King Hezekiah, who was uniquely excellent; he stands out among most of Israel's kings. Let's consider what made him extraordinary, by comparing him with Jesus, and see if we can make practical application.

> ***He trusted in the Lord God of Israel, so that after him was none like him among all the kings of Judah, nor who were before him. For he held fast to the Lord; he did not depart from following Him, but kept His commandments, which the Lord had commanded Moses. The Lord was with him; he prospered wherever he went.*** (2 Kings 18:5-7)

In order to walk in excellence, Hezekiah started by taking the trash out:

> ***"Hear me, Levites! Now sanctify yourselves, sanctify the house of the Lord God of your fathers, and carry out the rubbish from the holy place."*** (2 Chronicles 29:5)

The temple in Hezekiah's day was a picture of the believer under the new covenant. The outer court corresponds to the body, the holy place to the soul (mind, will, emotions) and the most holy place to the spirit. ***"Do you not know that you are the temple of God and that the Spirit of God dwells in you?"*** (1 Corinthians 3:16)

Is there any trash defiling your temple? We believe when we received Jesus as Lord, we were born again and made new creatures. This is the most important part of the cleansing process: the restoration of our most holy place, which is our spirit. God Himself seals our born-again spirit:

> ***"For all the promises of God in Him are Yes, and in Him Amen, to the glory of God through us. Now He who establishes us with you in Christ and has anointed us is God, who also has sealed us and given us the Spirit in our hearts as a guarantee."*** (2 Corinthians 1:20-22)

After cleansing the temple, Hezekiah continues to exhibit the characteristics of a good leader. ***"Then King Hezekiah rose early, gathered the rulers of the city, and went up to the house of the Lord."*** (2 Chronicles 29:20) Let's paraphrase: Hezekiah works hard and brings the most important people with him to church. He gets up early, demonstrating his diligence. Once there, he directs the preparatory work of the Levites, assembles the rulers, and goes up to the house of the Lord to worship. As leaders in the marketplace, we are to exhibit the same diligence and leadership skills. Diligence leads to excellence and there is no shortcut.

> ***Then Hezekiah commanded*** **them** ***to offer the burnt offering on the altar. And when the burnt offering began, the song of the Lord*** **also** ***began, with the trumpets and with the instruments of David king of Israel. So all the assembly worshiped, the singers sang, and the trumpeters sounded; all this continued until the burnt offering was finished.*** (2 Chronicles 29:27-28)

Sacrifice, praise and worship. Notice the sacrifices offered—the livestock—is the fruit of their labor. These were not family pets; livestock is literally life for the family. They use it for nearly everything. From a cow they get milk, meat, soap, and clothing. Sheep and cattle were also used as currency in biblical times, so for you to sacrifice the best of your flock meant you were literally giving up the things that your family needed to live. We also bring the fruit of our labor as a sacrifice to the

Lord. ***"Therefore by Him let us continually offer the sacrifice of praise to God, that is, the fruit of our lips, giving thanks to His name. But do not forget to do good and to share, for with such sacrifices God is well pleased."*** (Hebrews 13:15-16)

The atoning sacrifice of Christ alone makes our worship acceptable, for it is the only means by which we can be reconciled to God. We did nothing to earn it or deserve it; it is a free gift offered to us by God (Ephesians 2:8-9). There is nothing we can add to what Jesus did. There is nothing we can do to earn our freedom. All we can do is receive it as a gift. Then in response to that grace, in thankfulness, we do good works. Our works are a fruit, not a root. That is to say, our grace empowered works are a response of gratitude.

It's a matter of heart perspective. Whatever we lose for the sake of the Kingdom is not a loss, but an investment; just like when we take money from our savings account and invest it in something long-term where we cannot readily access the funds. We have not lost the money, we are just allocating it in a place that will one day bring a handsome return. In a similar manner, we invest our time, talent, and treasure in the Kingdom, knowing God stands ready to bless and multiply according to His wisdom and timing.

There is a story of how many years ago, a poor beggar walked alone down a makeshift road in the desert in India. As he walked in the heat of the day with worn-out shoes, he cursed the day he was born. His only possession of any value was a small bowl of rice. As he continued on in his bitterness, off in the distance he heard the noise of a trumpet that for a moment shook him out of his bout of self-pity and anger.

As he looked behind him, he saw a great procession travelling on the same road. It was the rajah, the local prince, sitting on his litter and being carried by four strong men. The beggar once again became overcome with anger at the thought of this young man travelling in such luxury, never having to walk a step in the hot desert sand, while he himself had to stumble along wearing old shoes filled with holes that let the hot sand burn his feet.

Soon, the procession caught up to him, and the beggar stepped off of the road to let the parade of men accompanying the rajah pass by, so he could continue on in his misery.

When the rajah's litter was nearly parallel to the beggar, the rajah ordered his men to stop. Then he motioned to the beggar to come over. A mixture of emotions overcame the beggar, he was fearful because he knew this young rajah had the ability to kill him in an instant; yet he was also filled with bitterness and anger, feeling life had not been fair to him as he continued to curse the day he was born.

Finally, he begrudgingly walked over to the rajah, clutching tightly to his bosom his only possession in the world, his bowl of rice.

The rajah motioned to the bowl and beckoned for the beggar to give it to him, saying, "Rice for the rajah." Shocked and filled with anger, he clutched it even closer to his bosom as he turned away to hide his face. He could still hear the voice saying over and over again, "Rice for the rajah, rice for the rajah."

Finally, in anger, he walked over to the litter and with a look signifying he was doing this under duress, he begrudgingly pulled out a single grain of rice and handed it to the rajah. After taking it, the rajah said yet again, "rice for the Rajah."

This was too much, so the beggar flatly refused to give up any more of what little he had left. How dare this rich young ruler demand that he give him his only possession of value when the rajah had all he could possibly need.

When it became evident that he would not give up his bowl of rice, even if it met his death, the rajah held out his hand and offered to give the grain of rice back to this angry beggar. The beggar took it and clutched it in his other hand, figuring he would put it back in the bowl once the rajah and his procession had moved on.

With sadness in his eyes, the rajah ordered his men to move on. As the procession continued down the road, once they were out of sight, the beggar opened his hand to view the grain of rice he gave under duress to the rajah, which had been returned to him.

As he looked at the tiny object in his hand, he was shocked to see that is was not a grain of rice, but a small piece of gold in the shape of a grain of rice. He then began to weep, and as he cried he said, "I wish I would have given him it all!"

CLEANSING YOUR TEMPLE

The excellence of Hezekiah's reign is a pre-echo of Jesus' messianic reign. On His way to offer the ultimate sacrifice, Jesus went up to Jerusalem (note *aliyah* means "go up"). Our Jewish brethren always say how they are going up to Jerusalem, regardless of the direction or altitude from which they are coming. The *aliyah* of the Jewish people to Israel in past decades is a particularly heartening, partial fulfilment of an important Biblical prophecy.

The first thing Jesus does upon His arrival in Jerusalem is to cleanse the temple before His sacrifice. ***"Then Jesus went into the temple of God and drove out all those who bought and sold in the temple, and overturned the tables of the money changers and the seats of those who sold doves."*** (Matthew 21:12)

Is there any trash in your temple? Any place taken up by fear, anxiety, depression, guilt, shame, anger, bitterness, pride or envy? These things take up important space.

Let's clear out the clutter in our hearts, filling them instead replacing it with the Holy Spirit, with godly prayers offered on our altar of incense, with our flames burning bright on the menorah, in our hearts making praise and singing psalms, hymns, and spiritual songs. Let's clean out the temple! ***"A good man out of the good treasure of the heart brings forth good things: and an evil man out of the evil treasure brings forth evil things."*** (Matthew 12:35) Out of the heart springs the issues of life. When true sacrificial worship is restored in our hearts, we cannot help but transform our lives. We will never be the same. Isn't that excellent?

Excellence is our relevance, our bridge to the world. The world understands excellence. If we are constantly exhibiting fruit of the spirit: love, joy, peace, patience, kindness, goodness, gentleness, faithfulness, and self-control, the world around us will be astonished. It may not understand other principles of the Kingdom, but the world values excellence.

The *talmidim*'s action plan for excellence:

- Cleanse the temple, get the rubbish out, remove the rubbish from our hearts

- Rise early (be diligent in our work)

- Constantly offer praise and worship to the Lord, for He is worthy; acknowledge Him as the source of every good thing

- Personal sacrifice, offering from the fruits of our labor; not merely tithes and offerings, but dedicating our everything to Him

What happens when we model Christ-like leadership in the marketplace? This is a vital question to ask because everyone is a leader and everyone is a follower. Regardless of what leadership position you hold, you are ultimately accountable to somebody or something. First, everyone is accountable to God, even if they do not acknowledge or even believe in Him.

Everyone in a leadership position is accountable to someone or some type of organization here in the physical realm. The President of the United States is accountable to the people and can be removed from office by Congress if he violates the Constitution. He is not a law unto himself. The same is true for all elected officials and judges. Even in countries that are not democracies, their leaders are still accountable. Just ask Robert Mugabe, former president of Zimbabwe, about that.

You are a leader in some area of your life; there are no exceptions to this rule. Regardless of who you are, there is someone who looks to you for leadership. In the workplace, it may be a new employee who comes to you for advice on the ins and outs of the company. You may not be in a leadership position, but that young worker knows you have knowledge that he needs if he is to succeed, so he or she looks up to you, whether you like it or not. If you have children, they look up to you as a leader. If you don't have children of your own, or if they are grownups and have left home, somewhere, there are young children that are watching you, even if you don't realize it. The point is: everyone is a leader to someone.

Many associate leadership with a title, but that has nothing to do with leadership. There are many people who have a title that are bosses or managers, but they are not true leaders. A true leader inspires people to want to follow them. The biblical description of a leader that is used most often is that of a shepherd. An American icon is the cowboy, epitomized by men like John Wayne, Clint Eastwood, Gene Autry, Roy Rogers, and others. However, as awesome as their feats are, these two occupations illustrate the stark difference in leadership.

A cowboy rides his horse behind the cattle and drives them forward. Many times, the cattle do so reluctantly, feeling forced to move when they would rather remain still and graze. However, a shepherd is out in front and the sheep willingly follow him, because they know they can trust him. This difference in leadership is expressed in the military. Those who have never served in the military generally believe the service consists of some mean person in charge, barking out orders to those under him, who in turn follow out of fear of retribution of some kind. While there are certainly elements of this, primarily in basic training when the drill instructors are trying to change a person's way of looking at the world from the perspective of a civilian into that of a solider, that all changes upon graduation from boot camp.

Think about it for a moment. In countless battles, a gruff old sergeant orders his men to attack the enemy in situations where they know many of them will die before they are able to make contact with the entrenched enemy. Yet despite this, they still jump off and move forward. Why? If you say they are afraid of the sergeant yelling at them, that makes no sense. Do you mean to tell me they are more afraid of being yelled at then they are about incoming bullets and artillery? The reason they rush forward in the face of certain death is they have confidence in their leaders, knowing they can be trusted when the going gets tough.

If you have influence on someone, you are a leader. You may not see yourself that way, but each of us needs to cultivate godly leadership skills so that as we move forward, others would want to follow. Even if you think your current leadership role is inconsequential, do a great job anyway; for it is the Lord we are serving, not men.

Joseph's leadership role in the Egyptian prison was probably not all that glorious, but the Lord built character in him and tested his heart. At the right time, Joseph was promoted from the prison to the palace, from interpreting the dreams of others to fulfilling dreams of his own. As previously stated, it is a clear biblical principle that God will give you a small amount of responsibility to oversee, and how you treat that which is little will determine if he can trust you with much.

In business, astute managers will often give a person a little bit of authority and responsibility to see what they do with it. They do not expect the person to never make mistakes, for that is part of the growth process. Rather, they are looking to see how the person will respond in their seemingly insignificant job. When they do an excellent job, it shows their superiors that they can be trusted with more responsibility and so on as they move up in the company.

We see this illustrated in the parable of the pounds in Luke 19. The person who was given ten pounds and doubled it was promoted and given authority over ten cities. Likewise was the case with the man given five pounds; but the person who was given a single pound and didn't think one measly pound was that important didn't treat it as something to be treasured and to be used to its fullest potential. As a result, he didn't do anything with what he had been given, and he had his position taken away from him.

In the Kingdom, leadership is inextricably linked to humility and service. Worldly leadership derives from cunning, skill, and fear-based control. As Machiavelli says, "It is better to be feared than loved." Not so in the Kingdom; true leadership qualities are developed by a servant heart as we imitate the servant King. Each of us is called to cultivate leadership skills to influence people for the Kingdom, whether in family, business, community or ministry.

This is why the world cannot understand true Christianity when it is practiced. In the worldly system, a person serves out of fear. Either fear of retaliation from the boss, or fear of losing their job if they don't do what they are told. The problem with this attitude is most of the time, it results in people only doing what is right or expected when the mean old boss is around. As soon as he leaves, they go back to their lackadaisical ways.

By contrast, in the ministry, even if you have a volunteer position, rest assured God is watching to see what you are doing with what He has given you. If you treat each person in your small sphere of influence as if you had a ministry of thousands of people, He will know He can trust you and promote you.

Hebrews 13:17 issues a challenge to followers to submit to their leaders, so long as they are following Scripture and godly principles. However, it also lists a warning to let followers know why this is important:

> ***"Obey them that have the rule over you, and submit yourselves: for they watch for your***

> ***souls, as they that must give account, that they may do it with joy, and not with grief: for that is unprofitable for you."***

In other words, if you are placed in a leadership position of any kind, God will hold you accountable for what you did with that position. That should be something that humbles, but also excites us. The example you set matters.

IMITATE THOSE WHO INSPIRE YOU

> ***"Remember your leaders, who spoke the word of God to you. Consider the outcome of their way of life and imitate their faith."*** (Hebrews 13:7)

Imitating godly leaders is divine wisdom, as displayed in the above quotation from Hebrews. This may be achieved both in studying the numerous leadership accounts in Scripture, but also and by building relationships with godly men and women as mentors. Attention should be paid not merely to sweeping motivational statements, but by the fruit borne in the life of the mentor. This is what is meant by considering the outcome of their way of life.

There is a well-established principle that if you want to be a success, get around those who are successful and learn everything you can from them. Don't just study what decisions they make; take time to find out why they made those decisions. What principles do they use to guide them in situations where there is no clear-cut Bible verse answer? The prophet Jeremiah said, ***"I will go the great men and speak to them, for they have known the way of the Lord."*** (Jeremiah 5:5).You will discover somewhere along the line they developed principles that guide them, which they use to prevent them from dipping their sails.

Good leaders exhibit passion and the courage to see a task through to completion. Nehemiah is one of these great leaders who applied this principle and there are many tremendous examples in the Tanakh. God put it into Nehemiah's heart to rebuild the walls of Jerusalem. Rather than just going off half-cocked, Nehemiah prayed for four months before he did anything. When he actually started the rebuilding process, it took two months to execute. The Book of Nehemiah begins almost 100 years after the first Israelite captives returned to Jerusalem from Babylon after their seventy years of captivity. Think of it: the walls were broken down for more than a century and nothing was done to fix the problem during that entire time. Attempts were made, but they all ended in frustration because those who started the project never had the vision or fortitude to see it through to the end. Then God put it in the heart of a leader to do something. Four months of prayer. Two months of work.

The battle is won beforehand in the process of praying and trusting God. While great leadership can lead to tremendous success, one is often confronted at the outset by the overwhelming enormity of the task and roadblocks that come along. We may think that we are not up to the mission, but God meets the need supernaturally when it's His plan at stake and not our own. That is why the prayer process is so critical. Firstly, in order to discern His heart and will on the matter. Secondly, to submit ourselves to Him fully, casting all our cares upon Him. When we do this, the burden is shifted from our ability and human strength into His supernatural depth of ability and resources.

We see this illustrated brilliantly in Ephesians 6 when it lists the armor of God:

> ***Therefore take up the whole armor of God, that you may be able to withstand in the evil day, and having done all, to stand. Stand therefore, having girded your waist with truth, having put on the breastplate of righteousness, and having shod your feet with the preparation of the gospel of peace; above all, taking the shield of faith with which you will be able***

> ***to quench all the fiery darts of the wicked one. And take the helmet of salvation, and the sword of the Spirit, which is the word of God;*** (Ephesians 6:13-17)

Most Christians and Bible teachers end the list there. However, notice the following verse 18 is a continuation of the list of a Christian's armor where it says, ***"Praying always with all prayer and supplication in the Spirit, being watchful to this end with all perseverance and supplication for all the saints."*** So, the whole armor of God includes prayer. There are defensive weapons, such as the helmet and shield, but also offensive weapons including the sword of the Spirit. I would contend that prayer in the Spirit is a key additional offensive weapon.

Let us notice what it says the weapons of the enemy are:

> ***"Above all, taking the shield of faith, with which you will be able to quench all the fiery darts of the wicked one."*** (Ephesians 6:16)

The enemy's weapon of choice is a dart, which is a long-range weapon. By contrast, a sword is a short-range weapon. In combat, a sword will do a soldier little good against an enemy who is able to fire artillery from afar. So what do these verses tell us?

First, when it comes to using the sword of the spirit, God intends for us to use it up close and personal. We are to go into the "highways and hedges" and meet people where they are. In the marketplaces, on the streets, in homes, in your local environment. God wants us to deal with people as individuals, one on one (Acts 20:20). When we have this up close and personal interaction, we are to use the sword of the Spirit, which is designed to cut through the hardened heart and move even the most stubborn to repentance (Hebrews 4:12).

By contrast, Satan is no fool. He knows the power of the Word of God, so he stands outside of our range and lobs darts at us while all we can do is slash at the air. His darts are a long-range weapon, just like a modern piece of artillery which can fire shells from a distance of several miles. The way to fight pro-actively against such a weapon is with our own long-range weapon, that is, prayer in the Spirit.

If God were not to give us such equipment, He would be setting us up for failure in spiritual warfare. So does He give us parity with Satan on this issue? The answer is yes. It is found in the phrase following verse 18 where He says we are to be ***"praying always with all prayer and supplication in the Spirit."***

Prayer is part of the armor of God; it is our long-range weapon and when preachers and teachers do not point this out, they are sending out members of their flock unarmed without all of the equipment God has issued them. So how does this weapon of prayer work?

Perhaps you're not fond of war analogies, but humor me. A great example of this can be found in the 1991 Gulf War, also named Desert Storm. Those who study the outcome of the battle learn it was a total rout for the forces of the dictator Saddam Hussein. Prior to the United States and her allies crossing the Kuwaiti border, experts predicted a bloodbath. They warned that Hussein's army was one of the world's most powerful. His ground forces outnumbered the coalition forces in tanks and the number of frontline soldiers. In addition, many of them were battle hardened, having fought in the Iran-Iraq war.

Yet, when the coalition forces attacked, the enemy folded, seemingly without much of a fight. Indeed, many enemy soldiers only offered up a token resistance by firing a few rounds in the air before surrendering, in order to save face and tell their leaders they resisted the Americans. The military experts said American casualties would be in the thousands. However, only 383 US troops died, compared to over 100,000 Iraqi soldiers. A ratio of nearly 30:1; a decisive victory. So what happened?

Prior to the ground attack against Iraqi forces, America and her allies bombarded the enemy with a thirty-eight-day air and artillery attack that consisted of 109,876 sorties that struck every military target including enemy Scud missiles, airfields, air defenses, electrical power, enemy forces, their command and control structures, and oil refineries to prevent them from being able to resupply their forces. As a result of this long-range bombardment, which the enemy could not successfully defend, the ground portion of Desert Storm only took three days before Iraqi forces surrendered unconditionally. The spiritual analogy is simple: thirty-eight days of air attack (prayer) and three days of actual ground force advance (action). This is a real war example to help us visualize what we must do in our *spiritual warfare*. Again, the battle is won on our knees.

This happened on an even grander scale during World War II. In the months following D-Day at Normandy, allied forces gained complete air supremacy of the skies over Europe. It was so complete that German military units feared movement during the day over open areas because they did not want to be spotted and subjected to bombardment. As a result, they would often hide in the woods and only attempt to move at night.

One such division was not so fortunate. The famed Panzer Lehr division was caught out in the open one day and was utterly decimated by allied bombers. The attack only lasted for a little more than an hour, but it is estimated that during that time, one bomb was dropped an average of every six feet. As a result, following the attack, there was no sign this famed and feared division had even existed.

In a similar manner, God has given us prayer to be used in the same way America used her air superiority to defeat the enemy. Sadly, many Christians wait until a spiritual attack comes their way and then resort to prayer as a defensive measure. Instead, if there is something you want to accomplish and spend large amounts of time preparing for, make specific and dedicated times of prayer part of that preparation.

Begin praying down the road for when the operation is executed. Pray God will bless the results then, even if is several months away. When you do this, you are essentially carpet-bombing the enemy. Notice our reliance, our dependence, and our trust is completely on Him. Our prayer life should be pro-active, not merely reactive.

There is plenty of biblical precedent for this. In Zechariah 10:1, Israel was told to ***"ask the Lord for rain in the time of the latter rain."*** What he meant was "pray for rain while it's raining." The reason is prayer is God's long-range weapon of mass destruction and is vastly superior to the measly little darts of the evil one. One cannot help but wonder, how many problems in our life could have been avoided if we would have only carpet-bombed them before they arrived.

Jesus said in John 15:5, ***"Without me you can do nothing."*** He spoke not just as a teacher, but as the leader of His twelve disciples. In other words, He gave them sound leadership advice. He warned them not to try to lead based on their personality or natural abilities, but to acknowledge their inadequacies and call upon Him through prayer, asking Him to be their ever-present help in time of need.

ANCIENT LEADERSHIP WISDOM IN NEHEMIAH

The book of Nehemiah is perhaps the ultimate "how-to" manual for leadership. Nehemiah served as the cupbearer to Artaxerxes, king of Persia. The modern equivalent might be something like the head of the secret service, entrusted with protecting the American president. Nehemiah had a powerful position and the intimate trust of the king.

This was a coveted job, but it came with many responsibilities and the possibility of great risk. One of the responsibilities was to be the king's food taster, to make sure nothing was poisoned. The only way to check was if the cupbearer survived, the food was safe, and if not, he would die. There was also a "rule" that no one could come into the king's presence with anything other than a joyful countenance. Bad news was forbidden and could result in beheading.

Nehemiah had just received bad news. A report came back from Jerusalem to Nehemiah that the survivors of the captivity, who repatriated to Jerusalem, were in great distress as the walls of the city were broken down and the gates inoperable. In ancient times, a city without walls and gates left its inhabitants exposed, vulnerable, and demoralized.

Nehemiah's reaction to this bad news shows the heart of a godly leader: ***"So it was, when I heard these words, that I sat down and wept, and mourned for many days; I was fasting and praying before the God of heaven."*** (Nehemiah 1:4) Nehemiah was devastated by the news. He had an important decision to make. He could never remain in the status quo; he became consumed with a holy discontent, which led to finite action. He had one of the best and most important jobs in the world's most powerful kingdom, yet he was willing to leave it all behind to go to a land that had been ravaged and attempt to rebuild a destroyed city. He would face dangers from robbers and would no doubt be criticized by those who would tell him it was a futile effort. There was no guarantee of success; this was not some small remodeling project.

Nehemiah could have easily been self-centered and written off the situation. Maybe he could have just prayed a bit and asked God to "send someone," leaving the problem to someone else, like many Christians do when they see a problem. No, Nehemiah's heart, like the Father's own, was bursting for his people and for Jerusalem. So much so that his first course of action was to face the king with a dismayed countenance. This was considered a criminal offense; he could have been fired, banished, or killed, but Nehemiah stepped out in faith and said, ***"Why should my face not look sad when the city where my fathers are buried lies in waste."*** (Nehemiah 2:3) Nehemiah displayed courage in approaching the king of Persia, but remember it was only after he sought the Lord in prayer.

So often, we get the order wrong. We call on the king, and after he refuses our request, then we start praying. Or we go to the doctor first, and only when he can't fix it immediately, do we start praying. Instead, let's seek the Lord first in everything we do, trusting even every minute detail to His care.

Artaxerxes asks what Nehemiah's request is. Nehemiah takes a massive step of faith and asks *big*, showing no lack of chutzpah. I love this. Nehemiah, who, just a moment ago, was cowering and so afraid, not knowing how the king would react, now asked for a leave of absence (which amounted to thirteen years), a royal decree backing the rebuilding project, plus all the financial resources and timber necessary to be paid for by at the expense of the Persian treasury.

True leaders ask *big*. They ask for the resources they need. They spare no expense. How much more should we ask *big* things when we go to our Father in prayer?

And the king gave him everything ***"according to the good hand of my God upon me."*** (Nehemiah 2:8)

Armed with the king's blessing, Nehemiah made the 800-mile pilgrimage to Jerusalem. This was also an act of faith, as a man travelling alone was ripe for attack by the bands of thieves who prowled the land. Immediately upon arrival, what did he do for three days? Nothing; and this is strategically an act of genius. After the long journey, Nehemiah first takes time to recharge his batteries before taking on the greatest leadership challenge of his life.

Good leaders take the time to replenish themselves physically and emotionally. He understood people feed off the energy of the leader. There are things a leader can teach you, but there are many things that cannot be taught. You have to "catch" it, discing those principles tacitly.

We have developed this attitude that a good leader works long hours and seldom sleeps. It is almost considered an act of weakness and laziness to take a vacation or sleep more than a few hours a night. That's foolish. We need proper sleep, good food, and exercise. We need laughter and fellowship. Even

Jesus had times when He would take time off from the work of the ministry for some R&R. How easy to over-spiritualize and miss the basics. It's our responsibility to replenish ourselves. No one is going to do it for us.

Nehemiah, under the cover of darkness, inspected the walls. He took full stock of the situation, discretely so as to minimize the pressure and PR.

It's important for leaders to have a realistic view of the present circumstances in order to not overestimate or underestimate the mission. If the leader is overconfident, the team can quickly become disenchanted. If he overestimates the task, the team may be discouraged.

On the other hand, it is vital for a leader to project a positive outlook, even in the midst of difficult situations. This does not mean he keeps his concerns from his followers if there are real challenges ahead. He should be honest when he communicates with those under him, but even in the midst of bad news, it is important to present it with a positive attitude and outlook. This may sound like having a Pollyannaish attitude, but nothing could be farther from the truth. Our God is still on His throne, and Romans 8:28 is still in the Bible.

It has been said, "Does it ever occur to you that nothing ever occurs to God." As a leader, you are human and will undoubtedly have moments of doubt when your faith wavers. This is just part of life, and God understands this (Psalm 78:39). Just as a good spirit is contagious, a scared or sad spirit will likewise spread throughout those under you, and can destroy the work you are trying to accomplish.

A military unit with good morale can take on an enemy several times their size and emerge victorious. Likewise, a depressed and demoralized group of soldiers, even if they are Special Forces, can lose the battle before it even begins. The key is to get an accurate read on the circumstances, and then plant the vision of what God wants to do. With that in mind, let us see how Nehemiah handled the situation.

First, the present reality: ***"You see the distress we are in, how Jerusalem lies in waste, and its gates are burned with fire."***

Now the vision: ***"Come let us build the wall of Jerusalem that we may no longer be a reproach."***

Team response: ***"So they said 'let us rise up and build.' Then they set their hands to this good work."*** (Nehemiah 2:17-18)

It's quite simple. Great leaders give an unvarnished assessment of where we are and then cast a vision of where we are going. The vision must include not only the *what* (build the wall), but also the *why* (that Israel may no longer be a reproach). People who understand these two things are far more likely to follow you with a zeal, for they know what you are asking them to do has a purpose and you have the situation under control.

Leadership is movement, from here to there. Invariably this includes resolving internal conflict and pushing through external opposition. Anyone can demonstrate good leadership characteristics when things are going well, but true character is revealed in crises. An example of that can be seen when Nehemiah's volunteer workforce was building:

> ***Now it happened, when Sanballat, Tobiah, the Arabs, the Ammonites, and the Ashdodites heard that the walls of Jerusalem were being restored and the gaps were beginning to be closed, that they became very angry, and all of them conspired together to come and attack Jerusalem and create confusion.*** (Nehemiah 4:7)

This was no small matter. The city was defenseless, and with the size of Jerusalem, it would be quite easy for a small force of men to find a way to infiltrate and attack the men doing the construction from behind while they slept. However, if they focused all their energy on fighting off the enemy, they would take their eye off the goal of rebuilding the walls. What to do? Nehemiah took five immediate and decisive actions:

- Armed guards were planted at intervals along the wall.

- Weapons were distributed to every single worker so that they could defend themselves if an attack occurred.

- A communication plan/warning system through the sounding of the shofar was implemented.

- The workers were reaffirmed this is the Lord's work, therefore, defending the work is also His battle. If we have to fight, know He will fight with us.

- Nehemiah set the example of being courageous himself by staying visible to all and by continuing to work on the wall. A sword in one hand and trowel in the other, Nehemiah lead by example.

The importance of this last step cannot be over-emphasized. By being visible, Nehemiah knew he made himself a target. The enemy knew he was the one in charge of this operation. Many times, if a leader is taken out, the rest of the team will quickly descend into a state of confusion, not knowing what to do next. This is why it is important for a leader not to keep his abilities secret, but be willing to train those under them to step in and fill their shoes. Ego has no part in successful leadership. In the Marine Corps, all Marines are taught they are to learn not just their own job, but the job of the next two people above them and below them. This is so if something happens to the leader, someone is available to immediately step up and finish the mission or project.

When people see their leader willing to get their hands dirty and get in the trenches with them, it is an amazing morale booster. One of the key complaints is that those at upper management levels don't know what those who actually deal with the public have to go through. This is why the best leaders are those who came up through the ranks and were once clerks, janitors, or some other entry-level position. Whenever a big inspection comes around, workers will often scramble to make things perfect for the big wigs who are coming down to see how things are going. The standard joke is, "We'll do things the way they want, then after they leave we'll go back to doing things the right way."

While that may sound like arrogance, and in some cases, it is, sadly, there is a grain of truth to the statement, as many managers have a view of things that is not grounded in reality. Spending time on the ground level can do a lot to fix this problem.

When a follower knows the leader truly cares about them, they will follow that leader to hell and back. When you inspire this kind of comradery on your team, you have a group that is unbeatable, no matter what comes their way.

When we examine Nehemiah's ministry and leadership skills, we see many amazing parallels to that of Jesus. Our Lord Jesus said, ***"I am the gate; whoever enters in by me will be saved."*** (John 10:9, NIV) Like the damaged gates of Jerusalem, Jesus' body was broken that we might enter in. Like the gates of the new Jerusalem, His body was restored, resurrected, and glorified. Indeed, He was delivered up because of our offenses and raised for our justification.

Like Nehemiah, Jesus left the splendor, comfort, and luxury of a kingdom to take on a difficult and thankless task. Our Lord ***"made Himself of no reputation, taking the form of a bondservant, and coming in the likeness of men. And being found in appearance as a man, He humbled Himself and became obedient to the point of death, even the death of the cross."*** (Philippians 2:7-8)

Have you ever sat down and truly contemplated what Jesus did to become a man, irrespective of Calvary? In Heaven, He was worshipped everywhere He went, and everyone showed

Him great reverence. He never knew what it was like to have a bad day, feel sick or pain, or be tired. All power was given to Him and there was no way He could be harmed.

He left all this to become completely vulnerable and live among us. He became an embryo in Mary's womb that needed to develop like any other person, completely vulnerable and delicate like all of us. I realize God the Father watched over Him all this time, but I am trying to get you to understand that He laid aside all the power of His deity while here on earth.

As a child, He was the same as any of us. Can you picture the creator of the universe, the incarnate Word of God, God the Son, crawling around on the floor and having His mother say, "Put that down. Don't put that in your mouth. Don't touch that"? I am not being irreverent, but Jesus had dirty diapers just like we did. The idea that the one who created the universe, who created you and me, would have a stinky diaper is beyond comprehension. Still, that is what happened. The meekness and humility of our Lord is astounding. As a child, He had skinned knees and was hurt while playing. While working in Joseph's workshop, He got splinters in his hands.

This is why Paul described Jesus' coming to earth as ***"the mystery of godliness."*** (1 Timothy 3:16) That is the right word to describe it: mystery. I cannot explain how this could be; I just know it is true.

By His doing this, Jesus can identify with everything we go through in life. Praise God for this! Unlike the gods of the world's other religions, who supposedly live in some mystical land and look down on his or her worshippers with indifference, never knowing what it truly means to be human and face the struggles we face like sorrow and death, our Lord and Savior, our God, knows exactly what it is like to be human, for He left His lofty position to come and be with us "on the wall" like Nehemiah did with his men.

If you are a leader who thinks you cannot be bothered to get your hands dirty by mingling with those on your team, let me say how arrogant this is. Jesus was willing to mingle and get His hands dirty, so if you feel this is beneath you, what you are saying is you are better than Jesus. I would not want to be in your shoes if this is how you feel.

Based on what we have learned from Scripture, let us examine what God feels are core values for godly leadership:

- Pray and commit the task to God.

- Know when to replenish yourself, physically, emotionally, and spiritually, just as Nehemiah rested three days upon arrival in Jerusalem.

- Offer the team an honest assessment of the present circumstances and clearly define the vision,

- Be courageous, just as Nehemiah was bold in making his requests to the king, and also how he disregarded the threats and curses of his enemies.

- Listen to godly counsel, and cultivate mentor relationships. ***"In the multitude of counsellors there is safety."*** (Proverbs 11:14)

- Do not be in it for self-ambition. Nehemiah used his vast expense account for the work and for the people. He used money for people, not people for money.

- Always remain aware of the opposition. Nehemiah works with a trowel in one hand and a sword in the other. Focus on the task at hand, but not myopically. Be aware of external threats (i.e. SWOT analysis).

- Lead by example. Never ask others to do something you are not willing to do yourself. Modern corporate managers delegate the dirty work, but Nehemiah rolled up his sleeves and got to it. In so doing, he won the hearts of the people of Israel. Nothing is more discouraging and frustrating than for a person to be working their tail off to the point of exhaustion, doing multiple projects all at once, while watching several managers just standing around talking and watching.

Prayer: *Adonai, Lord of Hosts, thank you for imparting this ancient leadership wisdom to me through your Holy Scripture. I pray the Holy Spirit will guide me into all truth, so that this wisdom, revealed in the lives of Hezekiah and Nehemiah, may become a reality in my life as well. Amen.*

Meditation X

Leadership: Team Building God's Way

> ***"Fulfill my joy by being like-minded, having the same love, being of one accord, of one mind."*** (Philippians 2:2)

Teams always look to the leader for energy and direction. Jesus said, "follow me." He led by example. The disciples could feed off His energy, His rhythm. The Lord was constantly traveling, preaching, teaching and working. After He sent out the *talmidim* for a mission trip, they came back victorious but worn out. Jesus says, "Let's get away to a deserted place," but the crowds followed Him and He ministered to them all, even though He was tired. Why did Jesus come to Jacob's well in Samaria? Because He was thirsty. We see the humanity of Jesus in His fatigue and thirst, yet He still leads by example. Even while suffering thirst, He gives living water. Though suffering fatigue, He continually gives us rest and refreshment.

Everything Jesus did is meant to be emulated. The tremendous miracles, healings, and words of wisdom revealed in the Gospels make my heart ache as I yearn for His greatness to shine through today.

Perhaps you don't feel you have the faith to see miracles, but the Lord will meet you where you are and your faith will grow as you hear the Word. God's grace to us is modelled as our Lord ***"poured water into a basin and began to wash the disciple's feet, and to wipe them with the towel with which He was girded."*** (John 13:5)

We can all start here by exhibiting that same humility in serving and loving the brethren. A few years ago, I attended a foot washing ceremony, where my pastor got down on his knees and washed my feet. I felt so unworthy, and the tears streamed down my cheeks as this dignified man stooped down before me. I still get completely overwhelmed just thinking about it. No one is worthy; that's why it's called grace.

First, we must receive His grace; we must allow the Lord to serve, wash, heal, and cleanse us. Then we are in position to minister to those about us. ***"For I have given you an example, that you should do as I have done to you . . . if you know these things, blessed are you if you do them."*** (John 13:15)

> ***"Imitate me, just as I also imitate Christ."*** (1 Corinthians 11:1)

> *The authority by which the Christian leader leads is not power but love, not force but example, not coercion but reasoned persuasion. Leaders have power, but power is safe only in the hands of those who humble themselves to serve.* - John Stott

When a leader exhibits these characteristics, he will not need to be a cowboy because the people will gladly follow him. While as fallen beings, there is always a side that wants to rebel against those in authority, it is also a characteristic of people to crave security. This comes from knowing there is someone above us who is there to reassure us and guide us. General Colin Powell, who was also the US Secretary of State, served under four presidential administrations. In his biography, *My American Journey*, published in 1995, he relates what it was like to serve under the former presidents. He said under George H.W. Bush's leadership, he felt like dad was in the room, which gave them a good sense of security, especially during Desert Storm. However, what he had to say about Reagan was striking.

He said it felt like the awe a young person feels being in the presence of grandpa.

One of the best secrets to being a good leader is "don't try to be a good leader." That may sound shocking and completely contradictory, but there is an important Bible truth behind it. Let's consider some of the great Bible leaders. Moses, by all objective standards, ranks near the top of a list of great leaders. He led over a million people in the desert for over forty years. Not only that, he stood up to the greatest empire in the world and demanded they let God's people go. Even at military academies, Moses is recognized as a great leader.

Yet, notice this was never Moses' goal. In Exodus 3, he tries to talk God out of calling him to be a leader. Moses never intended to be a leader, let alone a great leader. It says in Numbers 12:3 that ***"Moses was very meek, above all the men which were upon the face of the earth."*** So, what made Moses a successful leader? The answer is found in Deuteronomy 34:

> ***And there arose not a prophet since in Israel like unto Moses, whom the Lord knew face to face, in all the signs and the wonders, which the Lord sent him to do in the land of Egypt to Pharaoh, and to all his servants, and to all his land, and in all that mighty hand, and in all the great terror which Moses shewed in the sight of all Israel.*** (Deuteronomy 34:10-12)

Moses knew God in a way that no one else did. This knowledge caused people to want to be able to learn what he knew. It was this desire that caused the children of Israel, even with all their times of griping and complaining, to follow his leadership. Simply put, he had something they wanted.

David was a shepherd tending his father's sheep all by himself. He didn't say one day, "I want to be the king of Israel." Instead, he decided to be the best shepherd he could be. He was faithful in the little things, when no one was watching. That's integrity. When a lion and a bear went after the flock, David attacked the beasts in hand-to-hand combat. David had integrity and courage even when the cameras weren't rolling.

Most shepherds would just let the predator get away with an occasional sheep, chalking it up to the cost of doing business, but not David. He told himself, "My sheep trust me to be their shepherd and protect them. There is no way I am going to let that lion or bear take even one of my sheep without a fight. I don't care if I die; I am going to do my duty."

This courage carried over to when he became a soldier and he killed not only Goliath but tens of thousands. As a result, he gained a following, not because he sought it, but because he decided to be the best at what he did. When he did this, people naturally gravitated and sought out this leadership.

If you think about it, we see the same thing in the workplace. How many times does a person request a transfer to a company's branch or department because they have heard good things about a particular manager? They do so because there is something they have heard about that leader that they want to be a part of and learn from. Whatever area you find yourself in, try to learn as much about your job as you can and do the best you can at it. This is not what most people will do. Instead, most will merely execute the basic requirements of their job and have no desire to go beyond it. They may seek to be promoted, but their reasons have nothing to do with becoming the greatest in their area of expertise. When you seek to be the best at what you do and exemplify the courage of David, your superiors will fall over themselves to promote you.

This is what real leadership is all about, and when you practice it, people will willingly want to follow you, and you will not have to always be looking over their shoulder, wondering if you can trust them.

FOLLOW ME

Notice Jesus' recruitment pitch when He called His disciples. He said two simple words: "Follow me." Two simple words. The *talmidim* didn't need a long, convincing pitch. He didn't have to plead with them to come and join Him, or bribe them with a long list of goodies such as a health plan and benefits package. No, they sensed the charisma of this man who exuded the sheer confidence to say, "Follow me." A man with a vision and places to go. There was a palpable excitement flowing from His person; His presence shifted the atmosphere all around Him!

The leaders of Jesus' day said of Him, ***"No man ever spoke like this man!"*** (John 7:46) In other words, there was something about Jesus and His knowledge of the Scriptures and the things of God that no one else had. They didn't know how He got it—all they knew was they wanted it.

A great leader is also a great teacher. It does no good to know more than anyone else if you cannot pass on that knowledge to those you oversee. You can be a great leader in all the other areas, but if you are not able to reproduce yourself, then you will take all your abilities and skills to the grave with you. Or in the case of moving to another job, you will not leave behind the skills necessary for your department to continue on without you. This is why teaching involving the transfer of knowledge is such a vital part of leadership. You need to be looking for ways to impart small tidbits of knowledge so those under you will discover not just what you do, but learn why you did it. This will give them principles they can use to apply to situations that are not covered by procedures.

This is an especially valuable trait to pass on to your followers during those times when you are not available and a decision needs to be made on the spot. By reproducing yourself and transferring your knowledge, you not only exude a level of confidence that will make people want to be around you, you are also giving them the tools to succeed after you are gone.

Jesus knew there would be a time when He would no longer physically be with them. He did not keep things to Himself. Instead, if you examine the Gospels, He spent a great deal of time instructing His disciples to prepare them for how to continue on after He was gone. He sent them out two by two on missions. There is nothing more tragic then seeing a person create a successful company from scratch, cultivate a culture of success in leadership in every area, only to see that company fall apart within a few years of his death, all because the founder failed to reproduce himself to make sure what he created could endure without him.

A-level leaders recruit A-level talent. B-level leaders recruit C-level talent. One can easily distinguish blue chip managers from the B-level guys by the people they hire. A-level leaders are focused on the vision/mission. B-level leaders are all about themselves. They recruit less talented personnel because they are more malleable, easier to control and, in a sense, make them look good and feel like a boss.

What do you do as a leader to help cultivate a person with potential from being a B-level or C-level to an A-level valuable worker?

One of the keys to Dr. Jack Hyles becoming the pastor of the "World's Largest Sunday School" was his ability to recruit A-level talent. His ministry was one of the largest employers in the Hammond, Indiana area, so his insight in this area is worth noting. When training future pastors, who he hoped would go forth and replicate what he had done in other parts of the country, he told them when push came to shove, hire character over talent.

He explained it was his experience that "character will seek to obtain the skills and knowledge needed to be a success while talent has been known to flee character." He explains what he meant by two different employees he hired early in his ministry.

One of them was a man who had a reputation for being a top-notch talent in the music ministry. Although Hyles' church was small at the time, things fell into place when this man became available. Hyles was thrilled and hired this person.

Before long, friction developed between the two. Dr. Hyles had a vision for the type of church he was trying to build based on what he felt were biblical principles of music. He understood he was not an expert in the specifics of music, which is why he hired this man. However, the music leader started to make changes that were not in keeping with Hyles' vision for his ministry. He met with the gentleman and attempted to explain what he was looking for in an employee.

To his surprise, this talented individual pushed back, telling Hyles, "When it comes to music, I know what I am doing. You just stick to the preaching and other areas of the ministry and let me do things my way."

It was evident by his attitude that he was not going to submit to following the vision of the pastor of the church. His abilities in the field of music certainly made him A-level talent but he had his own agenda and vision that were contrary to those of the leader. Dr. Hyles was not about to go against his biblical convictions, and he was not going to tolerate a man who lacked the humility to submit to authority, so he had no choice but to fire the individual.

In contrast, during this same period of his ministry, he hired a secretary that did not know how to type. When it came to talent in this particular areas of expertise, she was the polar opposite of the music director. Dr. Hyles hired her despite her not having the relevant skills that some did; however, she had the character and desire to do the best job she could. After she was hired, despite having a family, she took night courses on her own to learn how to type. At the time he employed her, she would be considered by many to be C-level talent, but he saw something in her that he knew could be cultivated into A-level talent because she had the qualities of leadership in her that we have been describing. Unlike the music director, the woman ended up becoming Dr. Hyles' right hand for decades, essentially overseeing the entire ministry.

When looking for the best employees to surround yourself with, don't just look for the most impressive resume. While qualifications are important, don't overlook the potential talent that other leaders may be overlooking because they don't have the pedigree of others. This is what Jesus did. If you look at the qualifications of those He hired to be His disciples for His spiritual ministry, they were the motliest crew you could assemble. One of them was a tax collector, who in Roman times was able to extort whatever amount of money he could that exceeded the taxes due. Others were fishermen, who were dirty and stinky from being around fish all day. He called these men because He saw that while they may seem like C-level material in the ministry department, they had A-level potential. His instincts proved right. After His death and resurrection, it was said of these men that they had "turned the world upside down."

Prayer: *Heavenly Father, help me to be the best leader to those you have placed strategically in my life, even as I myself follow Jesus. Surround me with great people and help me to not be small minded or defensive. I believe my destiny in you is way more than I can handle in my own strength, so I surrender myself wholly unto you. In Jesus' name, Amen.*

Meditation XI

Testimony: The Explosive Power of the Gospel

"But you shall receive power when the Holy Spirit has come upon you; and you shall be witnesses to Me in Jerusalem, and in all Judea and Samaria, and to the end of the earth." (Acts 1:8)

It is a well-established principle that a person's last words are given great weight. In the legal system this is what is known as a "dying declaration," and is one of the few exceptions to the hearsay rule. It is assumed a person's last words are truthful and of great importance. This principle is applied to other areas of our lives as well. When a class graduates, they have a guest speaker who gives them the last lecture they will hear as a class, giving them a "charge." In the Bible we see this as well. At the end of their lives, Jacob, Moses, Joshua, David, Paul and others gave a charge to those they were leaving behind.

While Jesus is not dead, but alive, He did leave us with final words before He ascended back to Heaven. These words are meant to be our "mission statement" until He returns. These final words are found in the gospels and in the book of Acts.

And Jesus came and spoke to them, saying, "All power is given to me in heaven and on earth. Go therefore, and make disciples of all the nations, baptizing them in the name of

the Father, and of the Son, and of the Holy Spirit, teaching them to observe all things that I have commanded you; and, lo, I am with you always, even to the end of the age. Amen." (Matthew 28:18-20)

"And he said unto them, 'Go into all the world and preach the gospel to every creature.'" (Mark 16:15)

And He opened their understanding, that they might comprehend the Scriptures. Then He said to them, "Thus it is written, and thus it was necessary for the Christ to suffer and to rise from the dead the third day, and that repentance and remission of sins should be preached in His name to all nations, beginning at Jerusalem. And you are witnesses of these things. Behold, I send the Promise of My Father upon you; but tarry in the city of Jerusalem until you are endued with power from on high." (Luke 24:45-49)

The way of faith is not learning the rule book and seeing how much we can get away with. It's not warming the pew on Sundays as fire insurance against hell. No, our faith is all about pleasing God in a living, active relationship … ***"without faith, it is impossible to please Him."*** (Hebrews 11:6)

I love my wife and she knows that. She does. Does her knowledge of my love exempt me from showing love to her from time to time? Is it possible for me to say "*Je t'aime, chérie*" too much? Of course not. In the same way, we yearn to show God just how much we love Him, how much we appreciate Him just for who He is. Of all creation, human beings seem to fascinate God more than anything else in existence. He is infatuated with people … ***for God is love***. (1 John 4:8) Therefore,

I reason, that there is nothing He appreciates more than when we introduce Him to people!

As *talmidim*, we are called to witness the gospel in word and deed. As the verses above indicate, Jesus did not place any limitations on how, where, or when we are to share the gospel. He did not say, "Just share it and get excited about it when around other believers in church." He did not say, "Just share it with the homeless or the down and out of society," because after all, "they need it." No, we are to share our faith with everyone, anyplace and anytime.

Part of the reason for this universal charge is God knows we all have our own individual spheres of leadership that are unique to us. Our leadership in the marketplace presents us with unique opportunities to witness. Every day, you will encounter people that a pastor or evangelist may never meet. Likewise, a person who has any other job will see people in their workplace you will never see. Essentially, our charge to share the gospel is the ultimate in teamwork. If we all do our part, reaching those in our sphere of influence, we can all collectively fulfil the mission goal of reaching the world.

While works play no part in our salvation, there are many reasons why we should be a team player in this area. One of the first is out of a basic sense of gratitude. Sadly, this is a trait that is becoming more uncommon than it used to be. We should be grateful that Jesus is willing to provide us the ability to be saved from an eternity in hell. The Bible says in Ephesians 2:8-9 that we are saved by grace through faith. It has been said grace means unmerited favor. Another play on words uses grace as an acronym that says, "God's Riches At Christ's Expense."

Adam sinned in the garden by making a conscious choice to disobey God. We inherited this spirit of disobedience and all of us are sinners. Following the fall, God was under no obligation whatsoever to provide a way of reconciliation, for he was not the one that transgressed. He doesn't owe us anything and to think otherwise is the height of pride. God would have been perfectly justified in starting all over again, but He didn't.

Instead, Jesus, the one who John 1:1-2 said made all things, made a radical choice to become like His creation, and then experienced death in our place and for our atonement.

Jesus did this because this was the only way we could be reconciled with God's perfect justice which necessitates payment for sin. Praise God, if we have accepted Jesus to be our Lord and Savior and trusted in His completed work on Calvary we do not have to pay the ultimate price, for He paid it for us. This sacrifice was so great that He will forever bear the cost by having wounds in His body for all of eternity, while we will be with Him in heaven with a perfect body. The thought of the only imperfect body in heaven being that of Jesus, our creator and Savior, should cause us to be overwhelmed with gratitude that would cause us to shout from the highest rooftop what He did for us.

We should also be grateful for those who were thoughtful enough to take the time to share the gospel with us. We receive the gospel only because of generations of believers who took Jesus' mission statement to heart and passed it on to us. If they would have put their personal comfort first, the message of the gospel would have died out long ago.

I will be the first to admit there is a certain element of fear in sharing your faith. The devil will try to convince you that it's a bad idea. He will try to convince you that people don't want to hear, and it may cost you influence, respect, or even a promotion. He did the same thing with the twelve spies in the book of Numbers who were sent to spy out the Promised Land to make preparations to conquer it.

Ten of them saw the giants in the land and were convinced they could not win. Their defeatist spirit was contagious, and the people believed them over the two that had faith in God. Because of their choice, they were forced to wander in the desert for forty years until all those who doubted had died. In a touch of irony, when they finally went in and another pair of spies were sent to investigate Jericho, one of the greatest cities militarily of that time, they were told the people of the land had been quaking in their boots for forty years, waiting for them to come in and destroy their land. Listen to the words of a woman in Jericho who said this to the two spies:

> ***I know that the Lord has given you the land, that the terror of you has fallen on us, and that all the inhabitants of the land are fainthearted because of you. For we have heard how the Lord dried up the water of the Red Sea for you when you came out of Egypt, and what you did to the two kings of the Amorites who were on the other side of the Jordan, Sihon and Og, whom you utterly destroyed. And as soon as we heard these things, our hearts melted; neither did there remain any more courage in anyone because of you, for the Lord your God, He is God in heaven above and on earth beneath.*** (Joshua 2:9-11)

While it is true that not everyone will embrace the good news you are bringing them, many rejected Jesus when He gave them the same message. However, you will be shocked at how many will at least give you a hearing.

> ***Therefore God also has highly exalted Him and given Him the name which is above every name, that at the name of Jesus every knee should bow, of those in heaven, and of those on earth, and of those under the earth, and that every tongue should confess that Jesus Christ is Lord, to the glory of God the Father.*** (Philippians 2:9-11)

Another reason to share the gospel and live right for God is you have the ability to determine if those who have done so much for you will receive a full reward at the Judgment Seat of Christ. The Apostle John has something interesting to say about this.

> ***"Look to yourselves, that we do not lose those things we worked for, but that we may receive a full reward."*** (2 John 1:8)

He said to these early believers that he had passed some things along to them. After giving them this knowledge, he pleaded with them to think about what they had been given, because if they dismissed it or thought it to be unimportant and not pass on to others, John would suffer the consequences and could lose out on having a full reward.

Do you have a godly father or mother who sacrificed for you and tried to teach you to love God and do right? What about your friends who took time for you when you were going through trials and had questions about your faith. Do you care enough about them to try to make sure they get a full reward?

It may sound unfair—after all, why should a person suffer for the actions of others? However, this happens all the time. The actions that elected officials take regarding economic policy will determine whether a country experiences prosperity or recession. In Japan, the policies of others caused the country to go into stagnation resulting in what was known as the lost decade. The same was true in America with her Great Depression. It did not just happen by chance but was the direct result of the large movers and shakers of the nation's financial system. Let's not forget how the economic policies enforced on Germany by the Treaty of Versailles that ended World War I laid the groundwork for World War II, which was on a much more global scale.

Rather than focusing on the negative aspect of whether or not a person gets a full reward, look at the positive side. Prudent investment strategy always recommends taking a long-term approach. In America, critics of the stock market use examples of short-term sell-offs to scare people from the idea of "privatizing" social security. However, when you look at the long-term, there is a much higher rate of return than the current social security system that takes no risk.

I am not trying to get into the politics of entitlement reform, but I only use this as an example, for the same principle applies in the spiritual realm. While you may have short-term losses down here during your lifetime, in the long-term you will come out ahead if you make investments here and now.

If you are saved and living right for God, this is a direct result of the Apostle Paul's ministry, along with those of the early Christians mentioned in the book of Acts. Consider Stephen, who was martyred in Acts 7. By all accounts, he did not have time to obtain a great deal of fruit directly because he was martyred fairly quickly. However, his death was one of the catalysts for Paul's conversion, and as a result, Stephen is still seeing a return on his investment whenever a person gets saved today. There is a bumper sticker that says, "God's retirement plan is out of this world." While most people think that only applies to salvation, you can see how witnessing down here and following Jesus as his *talmid* yields long-term exponential growth that far exceeds the performance of any investment here on Earth. Not only that, you never know when your investment in witnessing will reap personal benefits presently. I can personally testify to the fact that walking with the Lord has improved my quality of life in every way. This is very important because as we testify to God's grace in our life, in terms of healing, deliverance, wholeness, prosperity, it points to Jesus, the author and finisher of our faith.

SOWING SEED INTO ETERNITY

Mr. Edward Kimball was a Sunday School teacher at Mount Vernon Congregational Church. One day, a young boy attended who was so Bible illiterate that he could not find the book of John and he would regularly fall asleep during the class.

Undeterred, here is the account of Kimball's using his leadership gift to change the world:

> "I started down town to Holton's shoe store," says Mr. Kimball. "When I was nearly there, I began to wonder whether I ought to go just then, during business hours. And I thought maybe my mission might embarrass the boy, that when I went away the other clerks might ask who I was, and when they learned might taunt Moody and ask if I was trying to make a good boy out of him. While I was pondering over it all, I passed the store without noticing it. Then when I found I had gone by the door, I determined to make a dash for it and have it over at once. I found Moody in the back part of the store wrapping up shoes in paper and putting them on shelves. I went up to him and put my hand on his shoulder, and as I leaned over I placed my foot upon a shoe box. Then I made my plea, and I feel that it was a weak one. I don't know just what words I used, nor could Mr. Moody tell. I simply told him of Christ's love for him and the love Christ wanted in return. That was all there was of it. I think Mr. Moody said afterward that there were tears in my eyes. It seemed that the young man was just ready for the light that then broke upon him, for there at once in the back of that shoe store in Boston the future great evangelist gave himself and his life to Christ."

That young boy's name was DL Moody. Today, almost no one knows the name Edward Kimball, but the many know DL Moody, the great evangelist who shook England and America for God, bringing over a million souls to Jesus Christ through his famous revivals. From DL Moody, a line of Evangelists can be traced leading all the way to Billy Graham. I would say that is a pretty good return on Kimball's investment to witness to this little boy, wouldn't you? Moody also returned Kimball's gift to him years later when Moody led Kimball's son to Jesus.

While there are many believers who share the good news for the reasons above or out of a sense of obligation or duty, sadly, far too many fall into the ditch on the other side of the road by compartmentalizing career and faith. They believe faith is something personal or to use a popular phrase, something "not to be worn on my shirt sleeve." If someone were to approach them unsolicited and ask how to be saved, they might take the time to share the gospel, but more than likely they will refer them to someone who is an "expert" in this area.

Witness is not a burdensome duty, nor is it something that we can ignore. I prefer to see it as a tremendous opportunity. It's an opportunity to gain ground for the Kingdom, and to secure eternal treasure in heaven not only for ourselves, but for those who had a role in sowing into our hearts.

Your childhood pastor, your mother, maybe a friend, all sowed the gospel in your heart; these all have a "stake" in your ministry. Think for a moment, who has sowed the most into your life? Who was instrumental in bringing you to faith? They stand to gain eternal rewards as you fulfil your kingdom purpose. Let's not let them down!

The gospel is raw kingdom power, pure and simple. To witness is to harness and manifest the raw power of God. His weakness is greater than our strength. He spoke and galaxies exploded across the universe. Each time we share Christ, power is released from the spiritual realm.

> *The gospel is this: we are more sinful and flawed in ourselves than we ever dared believe, yet at the very same time we are more loved and accepted in Jesus Christ than we ever dared hope. This is the only kind of relationship that will ever really transform us. Love without truth*

> *is sentimentality; it supports and affirms us but keeps us in the dark about our flaws. Truth without love is harshness; it gives us information, but in such a way that we cannot really hear it. God's saving love in Christ, however, is marked by both radical truthfulness about who we are and yet also radical, unconditional commitment to us. The merciful commitment strengthens us to see the truth about ourselves and repent. The conviction and repentance moves us to cling to and rest in God's mercy and gra*ce. -Tim Keller

The gospel transforms us. The world system is sowing and reaping, but the kingdom runs by grace. As we receive God's radical, unconditional commitment, we are emboldened to step out and even take risks for the Kingdom. I believe every time the gospel is shared, that unseen power is released ***"because it is the power of God that brings salvation to everyone who believes."*** (Romans 1:22)

Mordecai bore witness to God when he refused to bow down and worship Haman. Without a word and without regard for his own personal safety, Mordecai simply chose to follow the first commandment, ***"Thou shalt not have other gods before me,"*** (Exodus 20:3) which is echoed by Jesus in Luke 4:8, ***"You shall worship the Lord your God, and Him only shall you serve."***

With this simple act of obedience, Mordecai set in motion a series of events which initially appeared to threaten everything. Haman was not content to retaliate by merely humiliating Mordecai, but instead he resolved to wipe out all the Jewish people. Although Haman meant it for evil, God meant it for good. Mordecai stood by his witness. The result was that he, like Joseph and Daniel before him, was exalted to the most important position in the kingdom. Because of this witness, Mordecai went from persecution to promotion, becoming the most powerful person in the world after the king himself.

Do you have trials in your life? Are there things you're dealing with today? Count it all joy, my friend. God just might be setting you up for something greater than you ever dreamed.

THE TRANSFORMATIVE POWER OF THE GOSPEL

> *"Sovereign of all worlds! Not because of our righteous acts do we lay our supplications before you, but because of your abundant mercies."* (Siddur morning prayer)

Below is beautiful gospel allegory as told by Tim Keller, who was once my pastor in New York City long before he had published any books. I think it clearly demonstrates the transformative power of the Gospel.

> "It is said that one of the old czars of Russia had a trusted general who was dying of his wounds. When the soldier was on his deathbed, the czar promised to raise the soldier's young son and provide for him. After his death, the czar made good on his word. He gave the young boy the best of places to live and the best education. He was given a commission and entered the army. However, the young man had an addiction to gambling. Because he couldn't cover his gambling debts, he began to embezzle from his regiment's funds. One night he was sitting in the tent looking at the books and he realized that his embezzlement was about to be discovered. He could hide it no longer from the accountants. He sat drinking heavily as he prepared to kill himself. He had the revolver by his side and he took a few more drinks to strengthen his resolve for the suicide. But the drink was too potent and he passed out on the table.

That night the czar was doing what he often did. Disguised as a simple soldier, he was walking through the camp and the ranks, trying to assess the morale of his army, hearing what he could hear. He walked into his foster son's tent and saw him slumped over the book. He read the book and realized what he had done and what he was about to do.

When the young man awoke hours later, to his surprise the revolver was gone. Then he saw a letter by his hand. To his shock, it was a promissory note, saying "I the czar, will pay the full amount from my own personal funds to make up the difference found in this book." And it was sealed with the czar's personal seal. The czar had seen the young man's sin clearly, the full dimensions of what he had done. But he had covered and paid for the sin personally."

> ***For you did not receive the spirit of bondage again to fear, but you received the Spirit of adoption by whom we cry out, "Abba, Father." The Spirit Himself bears witness with our spirit that we are children of God, and if children, then heirs—heirs of God and joint heirs with Christ, if indeed we suffer with Him, that we may also be glorified together.*** (Romans 8:15)

See how liberating the gospel is. The young man could not stop gambling. He knew in his heart it was wrong, but had no power to change. True freedom is found on the far side of the cross. Only the *agape* love of his adopted father, the czar, has the power to break the addiction, to bring him back from the brink of oblivion and save his life. But the gospel doesn't end with salvation and redemption, as great as that is. The adopted son becomes legitimate heir to all the Kingdom. There may be inclinations and temptations from his old life that he will have to face from time to time. As he remembers the father's love for him, he will be empowered to reject his old ways. That's freedom. Not freedom to sin, but freedom from sin.

And even if we do stumble from time to time, we know that we will not fall. ***If we confess our sins, He is faithful and just to forgive us our sins and to cleanse us from all unrighteousness.*** (1 John 1:9) So if we are cleansed from unrighteousness ... this is important ... then we are actually *righteous* before God. How can we be sure? Because the forgiveness of the Father is ensured by His own faithfulness and justice. ***"Far be it from You to do such a thing as this, to slay the righteous with the wicked... Shall not the Judge of all the earth do right?"*** (Genesis 18:25)

Look at God's standard of forgiveness, as expressed by Jesus to His *talmid*, Peter:

> ***Then Peter came to Him and said, "Lord, how often shall my brother sin against me, and I forgive him? Up to seven times?" Jesus said to him, "I do not say to you, up to seven times, but up to seventy times seven.*** (Matthew 18:21-22)

If the Lord commands His disciples to forgive without limit, how much more will He adhere to His own standard? God does not ask us to do something He is not willing to do Himself. This is not cheap grace. Our sin is so utterly sinful that nothing less than the sacrificial atonement of the Son of God could suffice. He is our ultimate *kapparah* (plural, kapparot: "means of atonement").

> ***Oh, the depth of the riches both of the wisdom and knowledge of God! How unsearchable are His judgments and His ways past finding out!*** (Romans 11:33)

We are called to be channels of God's mercy. This grace we receive empowers and enables us to be gracious with those who have wronged us. We do not deny the sin, the injury, the hurt. We do not deny the ugly reality of sin, but we do cover it with our forgiveness, just as God forgives us in Jesus Christ. In commanding forgiveness, God is not asking something of us that He has not done Himself in infinitely greater measure.

And here another beautiful picture of the gospel, told by the noted Messianic Jewish scholar, David H. Stern:

"Once upon a time, there was a king who was strong, brave, and possessed of all other good qualities. He ruled his country justly, loved his people and was loved by them. Because of this there was no crime in his kingdom – until one day it was discovered that there was a thief on the loose in the land.

Knowing that wrongful behaviour would multiply unless he took a strong stand against it, the king decreed that when caught the thief would receive twenty lashes. But the thefts continued. He raised the punishment to forty lashes in the hope of deterring further crime, but to no avail. Finally, he announced that the criminal would be punished with sixty lashes, knowing that no one in the country could survive sixty lashes except himself. At last the thief was caught, and it turned out to be – the king's mother.

The king was faced with a dilemma. He loved his mother more than anyone in the world, but justice demanded that the punishment be carried out. Moreover, were his subjects to see that it was possible to commit a crime and not be punished for it, social order would eventually be completely undermined. At the same time, he knew that if he were to subject his own mother to a punishment that would kill her, the people's love would turn to revulsion and hate toward a man so lacking in compassion and ordinary affection, and he would be unable to govern at all. The whole nation wondered what he would do.

The day arrived for administering the prescribed punishment. The king mounted a platform in the capital's central square, and the royal flogger took his place. Then the king's elderly mother was brought forward, fragile and trembling. On seeing her son the king, she burst into tears. "I'm… so sorry… for what I did!" she wailed, between sobs. Then, recovering, the bent, white-haired figure made her way toward the flogging harness. The people gasped as the flogger raised his muscled arm with the leather whip.

Just as it was about to crack down on the exposed back of the woman who had given him birth, the king cried "Stop!" The arm poised in mid-air, the whip fell limp. The king rose from his seat, removed his robe, walked to the harness, embraced his mother, and, with his broad frame covering his mother and his bared back exposed to the flogger, commanded him, "Execute the sentence!" The sixty stripes fell on the back of the king.

> ***He was wounded for our transgressions, bruised for our iniquities;***
> ***His suffering was for our well-being, and by His stripes we are healed.***
> ***We all, like sheep, have gone astray;***
> ***We have turned, each one to his own way;***
> ***And Adonai has laid on Him the iniquity of us all.***
> (Isaiah 53:5-6 CEB)

Prayer: *Lord, I'm so grateful for what you did at Calvary. Thank you for turning my tests into testimonies, that I can live and declare your wonderful works. In your grace, empower me to be effective in communicating the gospel as well as the many testimonies of your love in my life. In Jesus' mighty name, Amen.*

Meditation XII

Sabbath: Living a Life of Rest

"And He said to them, 'The Sabbath was made for man, and not man for the Sabbath.'" (Mark 2:27)

Israel's *Shabbat* practice looked backed to God's rest on the seventh day of creation while looking forward to the perfect and finished work of Jesus at the cross. In the present age, the believer can rest in the perfect and finished work of Jesus now through faith. In the Age to Come, *Shabbat Shalom* will be enjoyed by all of restored creation, including the nations.

> By resting one day in seven, Israel declares the economic realm will not be the determining factor in their lives. They can take one day off in seven because God is the provider and will provide abundantly even if one seventh of life is given to worship, fellowship, and celebration. Of course, with the other designated times, it is much more than one seventh. When we add in Sabbath years, we see Israel was called to an extraordinary level of faith in God's provision instead of working in bondage to the economic realm. The Sabbath is proclaimed as a covenant sign for a way of life that honors God.

> Sabbath rest is a sign of the will of God for all peoples. It is God's intention that all be liberated from the bondage of slavery, both literally (externally) and spiritually (internally) from the soul bondage that destroys our peace and happiness. The Sabbath is a foreshadowing of the Age to Come and the universal Promised Land where all will live in the peace and rest of God. The Hebrew word *shalom* is a key term, defined as wholeness, peace, and well-being. By being reconciled to God and living by the power of His Spirit, we enter into the rest of faith (Hebrews 4). The Sabbath foreshadows one day all nations will enter into God's rest. Sabbath observance is an intercessory action for the sake of all nations, releasing the power of God to move history toward this goal. (Daniel Juster, *The Irrevocable Calling*)

The practice of Sabbath has always been a controversial topic. Many argue over how and when a new covenant believer should practice Sabbath. I'm actually not going to answer that for you. Rather, I'd like to delve into what is God's heart on the matter.

What is God's concept behind the idea of having a day of rest? By failing to ask this question, we fall into the common mistake of over ritualization. It goes something like this: a young man gets married and sometime after the honeymoon, he sits down to enjoy his first home-cooked meal prepared by his new bride.

She asks him to help get the roast out of the oven. He gladly goes in to help his lovely wife and upon opening the oven door, he is surprised to see the roast is cut in two pieces and cooked in separate pans. Curious, he asks why she didn't cook it in a single pan.

"Because that's the way my mother used to do it," she says.

The next time the couple visit her parents, she asks, "Mama, why did you always cook roasts in two different pans?"

"Well honey, that's because that was the only way to get it in the oven. When you were growing up, we had a small oven and it wouldn't fit in there in one piece."

In like manner, many of us have developed ideas about the Sabbath based on tradition, never stopping to ask the reason why things are done in a certain way. Instead, we focus too much on the externalities. Let's turn to the Word of God and ask the Holy Spirit what Sabbath means for us today.

Sabbath practice, historically, is not limited to one day per week. It includes the numerous festivals, such as Passover and Tabernacles. In addition, there is the Sabbath year, which is called Shmita, which in Hebrew literally translates to "release." Just as God instituted a day of rest on the seventh day, so too did he declare a year of rest, one out of every seven. This year of rest is consecrated to God, and Israel had to depend on His supernatural grace for their very survival, just as they received manna in the desert. God promised to perform a miracle of abundance, so that the harvest in the sixth year would be enough to sustain them through the seventh while the land lay fallow and was replenished. This was meant be a perpetual witness to God's role as provider.

During the Sabbath year, slaves were set free (Exodus 21:2-6), all debts within Israel were cancelled (Deuteronomy 15:1-6), while the land was not to be ploughed or harvested at all, but whatever grew naturally could be consumed by the poor (Exodus 23:10-11, Leviticus 25:1-7). What a beautiful picture of God's grace: supernatural provision and release from all captivity, debt and poverty. These are but types and shadows of what we may enjoy today under the new covenant with the grace of our Lord Jesus Christ.

In addition to all this is the year of Jubilee, to be celebrated every 50th year (Leviticus 25:8-13). Here is a double portion of rest and blessing, since the 49th year is a multiple of 7, Israel would rely on God's supernatural provision for two years in a row, both the Shmita on year 49 and the year of Jubilee on year 50. Note that Israel never really practiced Jubilee faithfully. In fact, there is no historical evidence that Jubilee was celebrated at all, not even once. So why did God institute it if Israel was never going to do it? Because all Scripture is God-breathed for our instruction. The rest of Sabbath, the release of Shmita, the supernatural abundance of Jubilee is all to foreshadow and model what we have in this magnificent *soteria* provided by our Lord Jesus Christ in His death and resurrection. Yes, Jesus declared it in front of his hometown synagogue when he read from the scroll of the Prophet Isaiah:

> ***"The Spirit of the Lord is upon Me,***
> ***Because He has anointed Me***
> ***To preach the gospel to the poor;***
> ***He has sent Me to heal the brokenhearted,***
> ***To proclaim liberty to the captives***
> ***And recovery of sight to the blind,***
> ***To set at liberty those who are oppressed;***
> ***To proclaim the acceptable year of the Lord."***
> (Luke 4:18-19)

Oh, hear the Lord's voice in your heart. He has declared Jubilee long ago and He is waiting patiently for His people to take it, to possess it, to walk it out. Not just one day per week, or one year in seven or one year in fifty. Perpetually. Agree with the Spirit inspired words of Paul in 2 Corinthians 6:2: ***"Behold, now is the accepted time; behold, now is the day of salvation."*** It was now when Jesus declared it in the synagogue at Nazareth. It was now when Paul repeated it by the inspiration of the Holy Spirit and, my friend, I'm here to tell you the time is now for Sabbath rest to be your daily experience, for the release of Shmita to free you from all bondage and debt. The supernatural abundance of Jubilee, the year of the Lord's favor, is upon you. Don't let His grace to you be in vain, take it now by faith in Jesus' name.

LINK BETWEEN SABBATH AND FINANCES

Let us consider the Sabbath from the perspective of what it can teach us about Kingdom living and our finances. To examine the Sabbath in this way, it is important to understand the circumstances that led to God revealing the Sabbath to Israel on Mt. Sinai (Exodus 31:13). This event happened shortly after the children of Israel had been delivered from slavery. Prior to this, as slaves, there was no such thing as vacation or time off from work. They were forced by their taskmasters to work as many hours as possible while leisure time was non-existent. In other words, work took priority over everything else. God literally had to teach them how to rest.

We see this also mentioned in Exodus 5:17, following Moses turning his staff into a serpent in Pharaoh's court. Following this miracle, Pharaoh decided to double their labors and forced them to make bricks without straw being provided by the Egyptians. When they complained about the added workload, Pharaoh responded, "ye are idle."

Essentially what he said was, "the reason you are complaining to your God about your condition is you've got too much spare time on your hands. I'm going to make your workload so heavy you won't have time to complain."

Sadly, many Christians live their life in such a way it appears they agree with Pharaoh's sentiments. In response to the welfare mentality, thinking we are being virtuous by obeying Paul's admonition that "if any shall not work, neither should he eat," many fall into the ditch on the other side of the road by overworking, trusting in their job or the economy, deriving self-worth from their title while forsaking their families.

There is a season when plowing the field is essential. There is another season when plowing is totally useless. Everything has its own time. When I was in university, I was working perhaps forty hours per week at Morgan Stanley, and then working another twenty to thirty hours attending lectures, studying and writing papers. I had times where I would sleep for a few hours under the conference room table after a full day of work then get up at midnight and start calling clients in Asia. It's okay to "burn the midnight oil" for a season, but only for a season. To be clear, the workaholic syndrome, though socially encouraged, is an ungodly way of life. There have been other times where I've taken up to an entire month off to be completely by myself, focusing on my health and seeking the Lord. Have you ever gone for a weekend with your phone completely switched off? I've done it for an entire month. No phone, no TV, no e-mail. What's the point? We must learn to discern the season by the leading of the Holy Spirit. It's important to flow with Him.

People may work long hours because they feel they want to earn money to support the work of the Kingdom. However, is this what God wants for us? While there are multiple condemnations against a slothful person in the book of Proverbs, do we have to go to the extreme to show we are not lazy? Isn't there some middle ground?

If you look at the instructions God gave for the Sabbath, it wasn't just the idea of taking a day off from secular work. Restrictions were implemented on how far they could go from their house and that they could not light the oven or cook a meal. The reason is, knowing the human heart, God realized if all He did was mandate a day off from work, we would find a way to keep busy on this day off with some other kind of work. The old joke goes, "Do you have plans this weekend, or do you own property?" Eventually, people tend to come up with cunning ways to circumvent the restrictions, keeping the letter, if not the sprit thereof. For instance, farmers might get around the restrictions of Shmita by simply working sixth-sevenths of the total arable land every year rather than taking the seventh year off. Good for the soil, but not the leap of faith God probably had in mind.

So, what exactly is God trying to tell us about the concept of Sabbath? I believe the idea behind the Sabbath, along with its restrictions is *God knows we need time to essentially bring everything to a halt and direct our focus on Him and our families*. Many of the problems in our western society can be traced to a single causal factor: absentee fathers. The principle of Sabbath is the most direct path for taking our families back.

As we mentioned in Meditation II, work itself is not part of the curse. However, following the fall, work degraged into toil because the land would now refuse to give up its bounty. What this means in practical terms is that there will always be something that will come up that needs to be addressed financially. Our fallen nature is such that whatever we have will never seem to be enough. Instead, we have the desire to build "bigger barns" (Luke 12:18), while we fail to pay attention to the "true riches."

We know we are commanded to work, and that work itself predates the fall. Yet how many people live in such a way that no matter how hard they work, it appears they never have enough? They may follow all the proper procedures such as having a budget, saving money, having an emergency fund, yet it feels as if their monthly expenses keep going up and they still have trouble making ends meet. To fix the issue, we start working longer hours, including weekends and missing worship services and time with our family, all in an effort to provide for our own (1 Timothy 5:8).

Consider a group of men working in a firehouse. Now, ask each of them for their job description. They would all say, "Well, to fight fires, of course."

Okay, fair enough, but they will not be putting out fires all day long. In fact, if you were to get the statistics for how many actual fires most firehouses deal with every year, the number would surprise you. This group of firefighters is paid a full-time salary so they are ready when a fire breaks out. However, there is a lot of time when they are not on a call, so various duties are assigned to them. One of them keeps the fire engine clean, one cooks, while another maintains the equipment.

Let's go back and ask them again what their job is. One will say, "My job is to cook the meals." Another would say, "Polish the pole," and so on. No, their job is to fight fires.

I say this because many of us would say, "My job is selling insurance" or "My job is managing a company," or "My job is repairing vehicles." Just like the case of the firemen, they are somewhat right, but their answers are not their primary job; the things they list are secondary to the main job. Our occupations are in actuality our second jobs. So, what is our primary job?

When all is said and done, our number one job is to believe that God can do His job. What is His job? To provide for us. Paul said in Philippians 4:19, ***"But my God shall supply all your need according to his riches in glory by Christ Jesus."*** So whose job is it to provide for all our needs and those of our family? God!

It means our top priority is to trust and obey God, and then to believe that God can do His job. I believe this is the essence of the command to ***"seek first the Kingdom of God and His righteousness."*** (Matthew 6:33) While you are about the Father's business, He's got your back. Can you give your load to Jesus? Can you let Him take the burden, while you seek His face? Let go and receive an abundance of grace and the free gift of His righteousness, for ***"all these things shall be added to you."*** (Matthew 6:33)

TAKE YOUR HANDS OFF THE WHEEL

To be sure, this is a scary concept, for it means surrendering control of your own destiny. Taking your hands off your own life. We tend to like to be in control, knowing how much money is in the bank, what we are expecting this month, what our long-range plans are to ensure we are financially stable due to our saving and investing, and so on. I am not saying there is anything wrong with any of these things. Instead, the issue is a matter of the heart as it is with so many other aspects of our faith.

While there are some things that are a no-brainer in the area of where a person's heart is, others are not quite so obvious. A person may have the purest of motives, yet in a subtle, barely noticeable change, can slowly develop an attitude of money worship.

Let me ask you a question, and please do not give me a quick answer. Instead, I want you to stop and take a good hard internal audit before you answer this question. Just like a detailed financial audit can take weeks, pray and ask God to show you the right answer to this question, *whatever it takes*. This is not intended to be a quick thing and then move on, but a long-term diagnosis.

Here is the question: What is the reason you are doing all these things with your money?

The reason I am asking you to do some serious soul-searching on the level that only comes from spending quality and quantity time alone with God, is I believe many people will be shocked at the answer.

Scores of articles have been written on what they call the "greatest transfer of wealth" that is about to occur or is occurring as those who were adults in the Great Depression in America, and their children who also went through that time, are preparing to pass their wealth down to their children. If you have ever known the adults who endured that terrible time in history, you will notice they all share a common trait. They have held onto their money, and never want to let go of any of it. I don't mean they hoard it and spend it on themselves instead of others, I mean they don't spend hardly any of it. They may have millions, but they are living as if they were paupers. The reason is that this time of economic crisis was so life-changing, they are afraid of this happening again, so they take steps to prevent it by keeping their money. Saving for the future is a godly thing, but an entire generation has learned to put their trust in uncertain riches and passed this ethic down.

This attitude is not limited to just those who have plenty. It is possible to be living paycheck to paycheck and still put all your hope and trust in acquiring wealth for the same reason; so you never have to live like this again. While at face value, this may sound like a noble goal, there is something darker at work here, something so deeply buried within. I believe many people with this attitude don't even know it exists. This motivation means at its basic level, that you are trusting in wealth, or the ability to never lose it again, more than you are in the God who gave you the wealth.

It is hard to identify this attitude because the symptoms suggest a life to be emulated, such as a desire to be thrifty and a wise steward with the money God has given to you. All these things God praises, and even commands us to do. However, when we unwittingly begin to put our trust in the security that comes from having this wealth, even if we use it prudently, we have established a false god in our heart and made money an idol. Because the way this happens is so subtle and insidious, it is rare that those who are so afflicted will easily realize the problem they have. This is why I say, please, for your own sake, do not answer quickly, for more often than not, it is only something God can reveal to you.

Again, *your only job is to believe that God can do His job*. I believe that is the essence of Sabbath: trusting God. It is easy to agree with that statement, but you can only truly believe it with the heart if you come to grips with why you are working to make money. If you are doing it for the wrong reasons, however noble they may be, you simply cannot fully embrace that statement about believing God can do His job any more than a person with blocked arteries in their heart can run a marathon.

The reason this is so important is, when you get to where you believe it is God's job to provide and yours is only to trust Him, it will transform every area of your life and how you view finances. You will begin to live a life of total surrender and dependence on Him. That's the secret. A life yielded to God demonstrates much more fruitfulness and power than any of us could muster in our own strength. This attitude is one that is impossible to have living in the natural realm; it can only come from viewing life with spiritual eyes, which is necessary if you are ever truly going to do something great for the Kingdom of

God. You must realize it is impossible, and you can't do it. Yet, God can, and He will.

CULTIVATING A GENEROUS HEART

One of the greatest areas you will see a change in once you see finances through spiritual eyes will be in the area of giving. When it comes to the area of giving, there are three types of people.

The first is the person who figures out exactly what he feels God expects him to give, then gives that amount but no more. If he believes in the tithe, he will figure it out, then take every "deduction" and "write-off" before figuring the amount he thinks he is supposed to give. Once he does this, he gladly gives, and he may even cheerfully give. Among these people are those who, after giving, act and feel as though they have done God a favor by helping contribute to His work. Of course, they forget that as the creator of the universe and of everything that went into the money they gave, God is not impressed.

The second type of giver is the sacrificial giver. This person always gladly gives to the work of God. When it calls for sacrificial giving, they will first figure out what they are expected to give, then examine their balance sheet and figure out how much they can afford to sacrificially give. This is not superficial, they will truly give until it hurts, and may even go without some things. Among these are people who have taken out second mortgages for the purposes of some sacrificial need they feel needs to be met, or even those who may sell something of value to them in order to give sacrificially. However, there is a line they will not cross. Not because of a hardened heart, but because they have crunched the numbers and know how far they can give before it is too much. While this is noble, and is certainly more generous than the first giver, they still are not where God wants them to be.

To do this, a person needs to enter the realm of the third giver. The Bible says in Psalm 37:4, ***"Delight yourself also in***

the Lord; and He shall give you the desires of your heart." Many people misunderstand this verse. They think if they delight themselves in God by enjoying reading Scripture, going to church, praying, and listening to Christian music, then God will give them the things they desire.

For a young Christian, God may do this occasionally because as a new babe in Christ they are learning what the Christian life is all about, and that includes prayer and watching God answer it. However, as we mature in Christ, the verse takes on its ultimate meaning: where God gives us the desires in our heart that he wants us to have. Have you had that experience yet? Where you look at a perfect stranger with compassion that you never felt before. Or perhaps you find your old appetites just fading away. Some of the movies and shows you used to love now are tasteless and a waste of time.

We come to a place where our desires parallel His own. If we are at this point, God will place in us the desires He feels He can trust us with and wants us to exhibit. Look at Father Abraham. What was the greatest desire of his heart? To have a son. Who put that desire in Abraham's heart? God did. Just as the deepest desire of Abraham's heart was fulfilled in Isaac, so too is the greatest desire of the Father's heart achieved; through the promised son, God would have a royal and chosen people for Himself, as numerous as the sand of the sea, to love and cherish throughout eternity.

As you move in this direction, you will arrive at a point where, just as you have desires for a certain food, you have a desire to give. Whatever God lays on your heart, you will give, because you realize your only job is to believe God can do His job, and that includes giving. You will not have to worry about giving because you realize it is impossible to do this, but with God, all things are possible.

The wonderful *Shabbat shalom* comes over us when we take refuge in God's character, as revealed in His divine name, Jehovah Jireh. True peace comes from resting from our work, and instead placing all our hope and expectation in the perfect and finished work of Jesus Christ. It is finished! Instead of merely sowing and reaping in a fallen world, you begin to just receive, what you didn't earn or deserve, because of your righteousness in Christ. This is a call to all believers to an abundant lifestyle of grace.

The Old Covenant parallel to this is when the Israelite's took the Promised Land: ***"I have given you a land for which you did not labor, and cities which you did not build, and you dwell in them; you eat of the vineyards and olive groves which you did not plant."*** (Joshua 24:13) It's a picture of grace, received through faith. Starting with salvation, but extending to every aspect of the Kingdom. We receive salvation by grace through faith, but that's only the starting point. By grace through faith, we are called to receive the fullness of His *Shabbat shalom*. Not just from sundown on Friday evening as a Jew or from Sunday morning as a Christian, but all the time, seven days per week, thanking Him for every good gift, now and forever.

PROTECT YOUR FAMILY TIME

If I wanted to, I could be on the road forty-eight weeks a year. Perhaps I could make more than I earn presently, but I often sacrifice my business agenda for my family needs. God knows that I can't be in two places at once. Many times I will turn down potentially lucrative meetings just to spend time with my kids. The Lord has shown me that my most important ministry is to my family. I don't have to chase after every business opportunity. And you know what? More often than not, opportunities seek me out, new relationships come to me. Blessings are hunting and chasing me down all the time. That's just what my Father loves to do because He is a good Papa. My job is just to trust Him and believe He can do His job. I am commanded to be the spiritual leader of my home, and this is what I am doing by showing I care about them more than I do about money.

The reason it is impossible to accomplish something in the Kingdom of God any other way is that if you think it is possible for you to do it, the more the world will get its hooks into you as you are doing things by trusting in your own ability and walking by sight. You are doing the same thing the person who came through the Depression does when they trust in what steps they have taken to provide for a "rainy day." Nebuchadnezzar made this mistake in Daniel 4 when he placed his security in his wealth saying, ***"The king spoke, saying, 'Is not this great Babylon, that I have built for a royal dwelling by my mighty power and for the honor of my majesty?'"*** (Daniel 4:30) Can you hear the pride in his tone? As a result, God took everything away from Nebuchadnezzar, including his mental faculties, until he realized where his security was. For seven years, one of the wealthiest and most powerful men who ever walked the earth was greatly humbled until he confessed God's sovereignty.

God never intended the Sabbath to become a ritual merely observed outwardly as a supposed sign of spirituality. Instead, his intention was to give us a way to realize in the area of our provision, ***"with men this is impossible; but with God all things are possible."*** (Matthew 19:26) By supernaturally supplying Israel during Sabbath observance, the Lord is demonstrating that He is the ultimate source of all our provision. Therefore, we don't need to work to the exclusion of all else, but rather to put our trust in Him.

WHAT ABOUT TITHING?

First of all, let me disclaim the fact that I've got no horse in this race. I make no income from offerings or tithes, which I think gives me a degree of objectivity on the matter. Secondly, and more importantly, let me assure you of this: as a believer under the new covenant, we are under grace, not under the law. It's interesting that the demands of grace are actually much more than those of the law. Whereas the old covenant demands a tithe of ten percent, grace demands you offer nothing less than yourself. That means everything you are, let alone everything you have. My view, after a lot of prayer and reflection, is the traditional ten percent tithe is a good general principle and starting point. We should certainly tithe. That being said, we are not condemned if we don't do it. You might say, what about Malachi 3, where it says we will be cursed with a curse for robbing God? My answer is what about Galatians 3? The Scripture expressly states we are delivered from the curse of the law because Christ became a curse for us that we may receive the blessing of Abraham and the promise of the Spirit. Thank you Jesus for a new and better covenant, founded on better promises. Hallelujah. ***"It is for freedom that Christ has set us free. Stand firm, then, and do not let yourselves be burdened again by a yoke of slavery."*** (Galatians 5:1 NIV)

You may then counter-argue that tithing predates the Law of Moses. It is absolutely correct that Abraham tithed a tenth of all to Melchizedek, centuries before the law was given through Moses at Mt. Sinai. Therefore, we know tithing is an important Kingdom principle and we should aim for it and more with God's help. Yet, neither let us be proud if we do it, nor let us be ashamed if we haven't gotten to that level of faith yet. Then again, circumcision also predates the Law of Moses, so there is a faulty logic in insisting that the new covenant believer absolutely must tithe since it is before the law. I don't see any preachers demanding you circumcise your boys.

Ah, the spirit is willing, but the flesh is weak. As you seek the Lord, He will deal with your heart on this matter. If one's heart is not right with the Lord, the one who fulfills the tithe perfectly will become self-righteous, while the one who doesn't will feel guilty and condemned. Thanks be to God, He has led us to liberty in His Son.

> ***"And I will rebuke the devourer for your sakes, so that he will not destroy the fruit of your ground, nor shall the vine fail to bear fruit for you in the field,' says the Lord of hosts."*** (Malachi 3:11)

Under the law, the devourer is rebuked for our sakes when we keep the commandment. It's a performance-based system. Make no mistake: the law is perfect, but we are not. Therefore, we can never make it. Praise the Lord, we are under grace. Therefore, the devourer is rebuked not for your sake, but for Jesus' sake. Not because of your performance, but because of His flawless performance. Grace is not a performance-based system; it is an identity-based system. Our identity is in Him.

Scripture makes it plain where our ability to get wealth comes from:

> ***"And you shall remember the Lord your God, for it is He who gives you power to get wealth, that He may establish His covenant which He swore to your fathers, as it is this day."*** (Deuteronomy 8:18)

We should strive to be sensitive to God putting the desires in our heart, and we will give not out of obligation, but out of a burning desire. We will have so developed a Sabbath mentality in the area of our finances that God can take us to new heights of prosperity. Instead of insisting on a legalistic system of tithing, I prefer to think of it as just investing in the Kingdom. The risk adjusted returns are out of this world!

REINVESTING FOR ETERNAL RICHES

An example of a person who has practiced Sabbath power and has lived the realization that his only job is to believe God can do His job is Dr. Russell Anderson.

Russell Anderson was born in 1913 and raised in Hunter, Kentucky. He came from a poor family back when the definition was far different than today. The family of seven was raised in a one-bedroom house with no running water or electricity. Two separate times his family had their house burn down and they lost everything.

As a boy, he started working in cornfields making fifty cents a day. At age nine, he wheeled sawdust for the local sawmills, and at eleven, he plowed fields with a mule for two dollars a day. In 1955, he took the first step to begin earning money by travelling with some friends to Michigan to work in construction. There, he learned the drywall trade and two years later, he started his own subcontracting business. Through hard work and God's blessings, his business began to take off. Soon, he realized he was paying over $50,000 a month for building supplies, so he started his own building supply business, so he could sell to his dry-walling business at cost. He made this business a success as well by selling to other construction companies. He later started a trucking business for the same reason.

From there, he ventured into real estate and began building apartments which he owned and maintained. At one time he owned 457 units, bringing in $45,700 a month in addition to the income from his other businesses. Adjusting for inflation, that was a massive income at the time. By all earthly standards Russell Anderson was the epitome of success, and someone to be emulated. However, he was like the rich man in Luke 18 who took no thought of his soul, instead focusing on building an even bigger empire.

In 1959, Russell Anderson realized he was a sinner in need of salvation and trusted Jesus Christ as his personal Lord and Savior. Soon after that, he learned about the doctrine of tithing. Rather than try to rationalize away why he couldn't give, he just assumed if God commanded it that was good enough for him. He began tithing and never stopped. By the time he was thirty-eight, Russell Anderson was a millionaire. Rather than keep his giving limited to the traditional tithe, he increased his giving to thirty percent. By 1970, he had upped his giving to fifty percent of everything he owned to Kingdom ministries all over the world.

Over his lifetime, this man has given millions to help spread the gospel and advance the Kingdom around the world. He made it his life goal to do everything he could with his money to reach people for Christ and make something of their lives for God. In 1999, he gave away over $11 million, which comes to $30,000 per day.

God has blessed this man immensely, not just financially, but also spiritually. As a result of his giving, an estimated twenty-one million people have come to Christ from all over the world. The uneducated son of a coal miner from Kentucky, Russell Anderson became known as the Millionaire Businessman of God. The reason is because he truly understood the vision of Sabbath power and that God is the one who gave him wealth, so he could do what man would say was impossible.

God is no respecter of persons. He did not intend for there to be just one Russell Anderson. Russell Anderson did not receive some special favor from God. No, God wants to do the same thing with you. The question is, do you have the same mindset as Russell Anderson?

In the capital markets, we refer to money as *liquidity*. The more it flows, the better the general level of prosperity for everyone. Most people view their income as a zero sum game. They think in order to gain, someone else has to lose. They view resources as a finite pie and all that matters is getting a bigger proportion of that pie. This worldly view can be summed up as, "Get all you can. Can all you get. Sit on your can."

There is nothing wrong with wealth *per se*. ***"Worthy is the Lamb, who was slain, to receive power and wealth and wisdom and strength and honor and glory and praise!"*** (Revelation 5:12) The prophecy depicts Jesus, who is the Lamb who was slain. Notice there are seven attributes, seven being the number of completion. I think of these seven attributes as "total *shalom*," multi-faceted, but part of one complete whole. This wholeness includes wealth, so it concludes logically that wealth in and of itself is not bad. If we have a heart to bless people and to meet the unspeakable needs, then we must become proficient in this area of abundance and good stewardship. As previously stated, the Scripture says, ***"A good man leaves an inheritance to his children's children."*** (Proverbs 13:22)

TRUE CAPITAL PRESERVATION

A man from Michigan suddenly came into a large amount of money by speculating aggressively in real estate in the years before the Great Recession in America. He became a millionaire, but his core values didn't change. This man was generous with his funds and gave hundreds of thousands of dollars out of his millions to his church to help them build a new auditorium, so they could reach their community for Jesus Christ. The gift was quite a large chunk of his net worth.

Once the sub-prime crisis hit, he lost nearly everything in the blink of an eye. One day he was with a colleague who was not a believer. The two of them drove by the new auditorium, built largely by his generous gift.

His coworker looked at him cynically, then pointed at the building and said, "Look at that. After what happened, I bet you wish you hadn't given all that money to that church."

The man smiled, looked at his friend and said, "I am so glad I invested all that money in God's work because I now have something left that is eternal and will never fade away. If I hadn't done this, I would have lost it all, just like the rest of my money."

Eventually, God blessed him and he regained much of his wealth.

That is the difference between the worldly view toward making money through our hard work and efforts, and understanding God is the one who gives us the ability to get wealth. One view is focused on the here and now and walks by sight, while the other places the emphasis on the eternal and walks by faith in the one who made all things.

Let's dare to believe God and step out in faith. The Lord has set you apart, He has called you by name. You are destined for greatness in Him. You may be just one proclamation short of your breakthrough. Stay in hope and prayer and faith and love. Yes, there is an enemy who will harass and oppose you at every turn, but you shall resist and counter every attack. No weapon formed against you shall prosper. By grace, through faith: you already have the victory in Jesus' name.

Prayer: *Father God, I confess I have been striving and working in my own strength. Lord, I repent of that. Lead me by the Holy Spirit from this day forward to live in your Sabbath rest and in true prosperity. I trust you alone as my source and my provider. I give you praise and thanks for the truths you have revealed to me. Help me, Lord, to act on the word. Speak to my heart and show me what practical steps I can take today to walk in the fullness of your abundant life. Even as I develop in this area of faith and finances, I ask you to send out many others to meet the great needs of the world and to establish your Kingdom in righteousness and truth. In Jesus' name, Amen.*

CPSIA information can be obtained
at www.ICGtesting.com
Printed in the USA
BVHW06s2256081018
529576BV00005B/176/P